MOVE RIGHT

BY JOHN HOWARD

A COMPREHENSIVE GUIDE TO SUCCESSFULLY BUYING & SELLING
PROPERTY, REDUCING STRESS, SAVING TIME & MONEY.

CONTENTS

John Howard is one of the most experienced property developers and investors in the UK today. During his 40-year career he has bought and sold approximately 4000 properties.

One of his most recent projects is a £27 million development of 150 apartments situated on the Ipswich Waterfront.

John was a major shareholder in Auction House UK, helping to make it one of the leading property auctioneers in the country. And this, alongside owning a number of estate agents, gives him a unique insight into the market.

'Move Right' will be John's fourth book, and his first that is specifically aimed at buying and selling your own residence. The goal of this book is to help people to buy and sell property in the smoothest and most stress-free way possible.

His passion for advising and helping less experienced property developers and investors has led him to launching the John Howard Joint Venture Fund, where he co-invests with other property developers and offers his own guidance and mentorship.

Alongside numerous television appearances and speaking appearances and seminars, John is the executive producer for two shows on Property TV, namely Property Elevator and the Property Graduate.

ACKNOWLEDGEMENTS

As always, when you write a book there are many people who have helped to get it to print and onto shelves.

A big thank you goes to my stepdaughter Ruby Howard who has helped with the editing of this book and endeavoured to make it as good as it could be.

Also thank you to Tiffany Howard who continues to help promoting and advising me.

And finally, thank you to all who read my last three books, and those who were involved in printing and distributing these books.

INTRODUCTION

Whether you are a first-time buyer or a seasoned property owner, this book will offer you advice for your first or future purchases. And with the right information I know you can enjoy a smooth and successful buying process.

My hope is that by reading this, you will save time and money. But most importantly it will reduce the avoidable stresses of buying property. Buying property can be an anxious time, with many saying that the only more challenging life event is divorce.

It may be the level of stress that results in people moving in the UK only every six and a half years on average. Yet, even if you meet this average, you could undergo house moves on five or six occasions throughout your life.

With some 60,000 to 80,000 properties sold each month in the UK, there is a lot of stress out there. Progressing a sale to a successful conclusion can be demanding, but this pales in comparison to the disappointment and worry when the sale falls through. Some 30% of sales do not continue to completion, and whilst this is not always unavoidable, this book will offer the practical advice to minimise that risk.

Buying a property can be considered a business transaction, compounded by significant excitement. This is largely due to it being a significant financial undertaking, so will always be emotional; particularly when you consider that people often invest many years of their hard-earned savings. Most sales are part of a chain of property purchases, with different solicitors, estate agents and property valuers involved in the process. A higher number of properties in this chain naturally increases the complexity for all of those involved, and in some cases can lower the success rate; although it is important to note that this is somewhat of an oversimplification.

If I can reduce your anxiety and make the process a little more enjoyable, as well as save you time and money, then my job is done.

This book has been written to cover many of the potential pitfalls, problems and eventualities that can occur during the buying process. However, my straightforward and practical advice that will help you navigate the, at times, challenging world of purchasing property, allowing you to achieve a smooth and successful house move as quickly as possible.

BUYING BLUEPRINT

Let's begin with a common scenario:

You've been considering moving for a while and find out about an incredible property that fits all your criteria. You book a viewing, and love it, and find it really is everything you hoped for. The next stage is obviously to put in an offer, at which point you run to the nearest estate agent, to get your own property on the market as quickly as possible; assuming you are not a first-time buyer.

After you have put your offer in, the seller's estate agent is obliged to report your offer to their client; the vendor. However, it is unlikely that their agent will advise them to accept such an offer, as you aren't really able to progress with the sale. This is the same advice that I would give to anyone selling their home, so you can't really blame them.

The only time I would accept an offer under this scenario is if the buyer has the funds in cash, or if they are a first-time buyer with proof of a mortgage offer. This is because generally if you haven't had a mortgage before, you won't really know how much you are able to borrow, or how easily you will be able to get approved for a mortgage. The reason I would advise against accepting an offer when someone has a house to sell is because the time between getting your house on the market, and actually selling can significantly delay a purchase.

Furthermore, you are unlikely to have a solicitor in place ready to act on your behalf, which is another thing that can take time to action and something that I will go into further detail on, later in the chapter.

In short, you should not be looking at properties, never mind making offers, until you are ready to act. You will have wasted both the agent's and the owner's time. You will also have set yourself up for disappointment.

Let's work with the possibility that you could sell your property instantly. You might even have a mortgage broker on speed-dial and you can look on Trust Pilot to find a solicitor in an instant. But, notice all the rushing around you are doing. You are about to make one of the most significant purchases of your life, and you are selecting people at a glance merely by a star rating on the internet.

Are you sure you want to put yourself under so much pressure by endeavouring to find the right person to assist you in this purchase in such a short time?

You could end up accepting the mortgage broker your estate agent pressured you to use, this financial advisor may then be limited to certain products and doesn't fulfil all the criteria later mentioned. And, you will likely agree because you are in a rush. You need to be aware that all of these people will be connected by commissions, so you need to consider if this will really result in you getting the best deal.

The selection of the right mortgage product is also a complicated task, with a vast array of products on the market. It is one that deserves a lot of research. You need to know how much you can afford to borrow and the mortgage deal that will best suit your circumstances. In short, without this knowledge of the details of your mortgage, you are in no position to know if you can fulfil the offer you have just made.

You may end up losing money when rushing to select a mortgage product if you are offered one. Your broker will provide you with a range of deals, but you won't have time to properly assess or challenge the selection. You may agree to the mortgage rate of least resistance and as a result, will end up paying more than you need to.

You may also find yourself tempted to put your existing property on the market at a competitive price for a quick sale. You are about to sacrifice a chunk of money because you looked at a home and fell in love before you were ready.

So, you made a hasty choice. As the saying goes, "Fail to plan, and you plan to fail." Let me guide you on how to be prepared for when your dream home does fall in your lap in the future.

PART 1

GET PREPARED

CHAPTER 1
GETTING YOUR TEAM TOGETHER

When buying a property, it's important to establish a team that is competent and works together to look after your best interest. Generally, this team will consist of three essential people acting on your behalf:

1. A Solicitor
2. An Estate Agent, and
3. A mortgage broker.

THE MORTGAGE BROKER

The first decision you need to make is which mortgage broker to use. And whilst speaking to your bank or building society is a sensible first step, many will only work with specific brokers and some will not deal with you directly. Therefore, if you have the freedom to select your own mortgage broker, researching the different options and choosing one with great recommendations that suits your situation is the best first step. Additionally, if you have a friend who has had a great experience with a mortgage broker, it would be worth considering them.

The right mortgage broker will work hard for you and your situation and will prove to be worth their weight in gold. A skilled and well-informed mortgage broker, like all of the three essential team members listed, can save you time, money, and a lot of stress.

When choosing a mortgage broker, there are specific details you should check. Most importantly, you should check if they are a 'whole of the market' broker. Some brokers are tied to a leading organisation. Your first question should be 'Do you have a whole of market approach?' If the answer is no, find one that says yes.

You also need to ask if they charge broker's fees. It is totally and utterly unnecessary to pay broker's fees, as they get paid a commission from the building society or lending institution that they choose to recommend to you. Therefore, you should choose the broker who offers the services with no additional charge payable by you. This is certainly an area where paying more will not ensure a better service, there are plenty of excellent brokers who will not charge you.

The best mortgage brokers will help you navigate the small print of a mortgage deal. There are currently so many products on the market that anyone would be forgiven for being overwhelmed. A mortgage broker will find you the right products with the lowest interest rate. They will present you with fixed-term deals, whether two-years or five-years and help you to understand the consequences of your choice.

The mortgage broker should make you aware that the rate may rise significantly higher after the fixed term period, as opposed to the initial rate offered. They should also make you aware of the penalties for paying off the mortgage early or swapping to a different product. A good broker will also promise to contact you at the end of the fixed term to help you seek a better deal with another company. This is not an act of charity on the part of the broker, as he or she will receive a commission from the new lending organisation.

Remember, you are drawing together a team for a reason. Even though you have sought advice from the mortgage broker, you should ask your solicitor to read through the paper work before you sign it.

The estate agent may also encourage you to see an in-house mortgage broker. Try to avoid being bullied into using this broker if you do not wish to. Although some in-house brokers are excellent and, as always, you should receive assurance that they can view the whole market, as you need access to the best rates. If you do choose to use an in-house mortgage broker, you should consider all the same criteria as previously mentioned.

Estate agency has changed dramatically over the last few years, so it isn't surprising that an estate agent will want you to use their broker. A lot of agencies now only make a profit thanks to the business undertaken by their mortgage broker and property management services. Therefore, they will try to put immense pressure on you to use this service for this reason.

Some agencies may go so far as to not let you view a property until you have an appointment with the in-house broker. They will state that this is so that they can be sure that you can afford to pay for the property you are viewing. You can argue that this is good practice, as you could be wasting their time. However, even if you see the broker, you are not compelled to use the service. Therefore, if there is a property that you are really keen to view, it may be worth making an appointment with their mortgage broker just to enable you to do so.

When dealing with your chosen mortgage broker, you must be totally honest about all of your debt. Please do not try to hide any misdemeanours from your past, as they will come to light. Any dishonesty will lead to your mortgage being refused and you being forced to start again from the beginning with a different lender.

If you have had financial problems in the past, you need to be totally honest as they will be discovered anyway. If you fear this means you will not get a mortgage, it is not the case that all hope is lost. Several financial institutions may still lend to you, even if they ask for a higher interest rate, but they will still allow you to borrow money in many cases.

Your mortgage broker will be able to find you a mortgage somewhere in the market. If they can't find you a product, then they are not the best in the profession, and you should seek a different broker. We are incredibly lucky in the UK. There are so many building societies and other lending institutions willing to lend money on property at a low-interest rate. The UK is almost unique in the world, and it makes our property market attractive, especially as there is currently no tax when you sell your main residence.

THE SOLICITOR

I always consider solicitors to be a necessary evil. This sounds pretty harsh, considering they have helped me to become successful over the years. I have one solicitor who I have used for nearly thirty years: Mark Hayward of Hayward Moon. I trust him implicitly with everything I do. If he says I shouldn't do a deal, then I don't do it. However, as you are not buying and selling regularly, you probably won't be as fortunate as to have this special relationship.

Having said this, you must have a good rapport with your solicitor. You need to feel you can get hold of them when you need to. If they give you the feeling that they are doing you a favour when they return your call after five days, this is unacceptable.

I want to talk you through the rules I present during my seminars and the advice I give about choosing a solicitor. If you opt for a licensed conveyancer, you should still follow these rules. A solicitor is a more general term, and can apply to all areas of law, whereas a licensed conveyancer will only deal with property. From this point forward, I will use the term solicitor to cover both.

Rule 1: Always ask the solicitor if they are about to go on holiday or if they work full-time or part-time. It is essential that your solicitor is full time and will be available throughout the conveyancing process. You also need to be assured that they will not move firms during this time.

Rule 2: In my experience, you really do need to be able to go and see your solicitor, so choose a local one. However, I appreciate there are exceptions to this rule, especially with the power of emails and video conferencing, such as Skype.

Rule 3: Please do not pick a solicitor that is online only. The temptation will be high, as they are often cheaper than a traditional solicitor. But, as with many things, there is a reason they are cheaper; they do not come with a good reputation, and some agents and solicitors refuse to work with them.

Rule 4: Do not choose a solicitor based on price. The costs break my heart as much as they will yours. Yet, solicitors do an essential job, and you need them to get it right. Make sure you negotiate a fixed price for doing the job. Do not accept a vague answer when you ask about costs. When they offer their set price, check how much their disbursements will be.

These disbursements will be added onto your bill and include such things as dealing with the mortgage, carrying out local searches, and so on. You must demand a total figure for the solicitor's services so that you are able to work out your finances accurately.

With these rules in mind, it is time to reach out to solicitors. When seeking your solicitor, you should take a recommendation from someone else. Many estate agents will recommend a solicitor, though there will be reasons they do this. It might be that they get a commission for the referral. More likely, they will choose a solicitor that they know will act quickly and efficiently. If the solicitor values this recommendation, they will likely make every effort to make sure your transaction goes through smoothly. They will want more recommendations from the estate agent. Therefore, this is not a bad thing for you.

You should also ask the solicitor to explain the level of transparency within the firm. Many solicitors are now able share legal files online with other parties involved in the transaction and this is excellent news.

In my experience, there is no reason why a purchase should take more than twenty-eight days if both parties are able and willing to proceed quickly. One way to make sure you speed up the process is to ask the solicitor to proceed with the local searches[1] on the property as soon as you have instructed them. This is a quick trick that makes a huge difference. The searches can be time-consuming, as your solicitor applies to the local authority for answers to a set of questions. They will want to know things such as information about new roads, or indeed anything detrimental that might impact on the purchase of your property. There might be legal orders on the property or issues with noise abatement or environmental problems. Some searches will take the full month and can slow the transaction dramatically. No lending institution will lend you money without the local searches being acceptable.

Your solicitor might want to wait until you have your mortgage offer before doing these searches. The reason to wait is to save you money. If there is a problem with your mortgage offer, the sale may be aborted. However, in my view, this is a 'no guts, no glory' decision. Too much time taken during the deal is the primary reason for owners to pull out of the sale.

As this is so vital to the progression of the sale, instructing them to start early with the searches is essential. It is also a good test to see how helpful and positive your solicitor is going to be moving forward.

---

1   A local search is carried out by the local authority. Lenders require local searches to ensure that there is nothing that will affect the value of the property, but they also ensure that there isn't anything which will interfere with your use or enjoyment.

CHAPTER 2

WAYS OF BUYING AND SELLING PROPERTY

TRADITIONAL ESTATE AGENTS

There are currently around 16,500 estate agents in the UK, and they represent most of the property that is for sale publicly in the country.

The traditional estate agent has a mixed reputation. First, there are corporate agents. These estate agents own multiple practices across the UK and come with a reputation for being sharp and on the ball. Then, there is the small, local, independent estate agent, who is often considered easier and less pushy.

You may deal with either sort of estate agent, as it all depends on who is marketing the property for sale that you want to buy. All agents will be keen to sell to you if you are in a position to proceed.

Most property sold through an estate agent will be sold 'Subject to Contract'. Basically, this means you agree to purchase the property subject to the details in the contract and dependent on the legal enquiries made by your solicitor on your behalf.

The process is simple. You view the property, you make the offer, you instruct your solicitors and depending on what they come back and say, you go ahead and purchase the property. The success of this process will depend on the legal work and the availability of a mortgage.

ONLINE ESTATE AGENTS

Using an online estate agent offers the potential for reducing costs, as the agent doesn't have an office and all the attending overheads of the traditional estate agent. However, my personal experience of online estate agents has been one of problems. Often, the seller will want too much money for the property and will want to pay as little commission as possible. Most traditional estate agents avoid these clients, as they are generally wasting everyone's time.

If you are buying from an online agent, you will end up doing a lot of the leg work yourself. Most online agents are paid commission upfront and have no incentive to get the sale through to completion. It will become clear that finding a buyer is only the start of the process. Driving a transaction through to completion takes a lot of hard work.

As state previously, they won't be concerned with what the sale price is, as they have already had their commission. The seller will have paid a one-off fee and will be reluctant to go to a traditional estate agent and pay another. It is likely they should have gone to the traditional estate agent in the first place and got the job done correctly from the start.

PRIVATE SALES

The person who thinks they know better than an estate agent is an interesting one. They believe they can get more money for their property and will not have to pay the commission. The reality will likely be very different!

They will start off thinking they can do it all for themselves but will eventually approach an estate agent to sell the property. It is likely it will have been on the market for a long time before this happens, and they will end up getting less than if they had gone to the estate agent in the first place.

CHAPTER 3

WORKING WITH ESTATE AGENTS

Having secured a mortgage broker and solicitor, you are now ready to start the exciting part: cutting a deal with the estate agent.

The reputation enjoyed by estate agents isn't the best amongst the public, with many viewing them as another necessary evil in the process of buying and selling property. As I used to be one, and now own estate agencies, I have a better understanding of these professionals than most people. I understand what motivates them and how to get the best service; whether you are buying or selling.

You may hold the misconception that the agent is out to get the highest price possible for the property. Most agents indeed get a higher commission the more they sell the house for. However, the difference in commission between a property at £200,000 compared to £220,000 is negligible. Ultimately, it is in the best interest of the estate agent to sell your property for whatever price they can get.

It is the speed of sales that keeps the business going. Most agents have a conscience and will definitely work to get the best price for the client. I would be disappointed if one of my team did anything but battle for the best price for our clients.

Essentially, the role of an estate agent is one of compromise. When you understand this, it is much easier to work with them. The vast majority are the type of people that wake up and hope for a sunny day, as they then know it will be easier to sell property.

It is important to debunk these myths surrounding the reputation of estate agents as knowing the truth will help you to understand the right approach to cutting the best deal with these property experts.

Understanding that estate agents are generally optimistic people who hate delivering lousy news helps you build good rapport with them. Working well with the agent is essential if you want to enjoy a successful purchase. Imagine you are an estate agent and the most fantastic property arrives on your desk. Who will you contact first? The grumpy potential purchaser or the courteous, serious buyer who seems to like you and spends time getting to know you? Being kind, charming and engaging is the easiest way to get to the front of the queue.

Then, when you have put in an offer on a property, a positive relationship with the agent is even more important. You want the deal to progress smoothly with as few challenges as possible. The person who will overcome any problems is likely to be the estate agent, as they will be in contact with the current owner asking questions on your behalf.

The larger and better quality estate agents will have a sales progression team. As the name suggests, this team does the onerous task of working with clients from offer to completion. Getting an offer is about 30% of the job while moving it to completion is the other 70%. A sale that falls through means the process must start over again. Thus, this team will monitor and drive the sale forwards; they will unblock any obstacles and liaise between both sets of solicitors, the vendor, and the buyer.

Once a sale has been agreed, you should ask to be introduced to the team member from the sales progression department who will be responsible for your purchase. You will learn to love them, and you are likely to pass your flowers and thank you cards in their direction. The sales negotiator used to get the plaudits – but how times have changed – the sales progression team secures the deal and gets the pat on the back.

Remember, it is in everyone's interest to get the sale to completion quickly. Therefore, you should expect weekly updates from your sales progressor. You should not be embarrassed or apologetic for chasing them up. They will get the commission quicker and an eager, organised client is better for them too.

The longer the sale goes on, the more risk there is that it won't happen. Therefore, the agent should be keen to avoid a lost sale, as running an estate agents is an expensive business and they don't get paid if the sale falls through. If the sale falls through, then a seller is able to choose a different agency moving forward, and they will have wasted their own time and money. Therefore, you should feel no embarrassment at ringing them up and asking for progress; a proactive buyer is certainly helping them.

CHAPTER 4
LET'S GET LEGAL

When it comes to buying a home, there is a lot of legal jargon used by solicitors. It will definitely be useful to have a full understanding of this language when it comes to buying or selling a home, as these are generally terms that you will not have come across in everyday life.

For both my sake and yours, I will keep this chapter brief.

FREEHOLD TITLE

The freeholder of a property owns it outright, and this includes the land that the property is built on. As an owner of the freehold title you are responsible for maintaining your property and the land. This means that you will need to budget for these costs. Most houses are freehold, however in the north of England it used to be relatively common for houses to be leasehold but if you come across one now I would certainly look into why this would be the case. It a house is leasehold nowadays it is normally because it is part of a shared ownership scheme.

ABSOLUTE TITLE

This term will also be used by solicitors and can be used interchangeably for freehold title.

POSSESSORY TITLE

A possessory title refers to the ownership of land by someone who does not have deeds to document their ownership, because those documents do not exist; they have been lost or destroyed.

However, if you are buying a property and your solicitor says that the owner has a possessory title you can normally insure against the problem and it won't cost a lot of money under normal circumstances to do so. This insures against the possibility of a claim on ownership from someone else.

Additionally, in most cases the owner will pay for this insurance prior to your purchase.

LEASEHOLD TITLE

A leasehold title is held by an owner for a term specified in the lease, normally between 99 years and 999 years. This is the defining difference between a leasehold and a freehold title; a freehold title continues forever. And this refers to the length of time that the occupier is granted the right to occupy the property by the freeholder. There can be multiple leasehold titles under one freehold title.

At the end of the lease the property returns to the full possession of the freeholder. Of course, in reality this never really happens anymore because once the lease is down to much less than 99 years it is renewed under the Leasehold Reform Act 1967.

COVENANT

When you are purchasing an older property, it is far more likely to have a covenant on the title. However, it is worth noting here that a leasehold title can also be subject to covenants. These normally stop you from carrying out certain activities at the property. Quite often called restrictive covenants, they prevent the landowner from doing certain things. For instance, building more property on the land or selling alcohol.

If a restrictive covenant is old, normally over 50 years, then there is a good chance that you'll be able to insure against anyone coming forward and stopping you from doing these activities. Some insurance companies specialise in this and the premiums are generally in the hundreds, not thousands; and a solicitor will organise this if required.

If the covenant has not been on the property very long, then there is a good chance that it can't be insured against. Although, if the person who has put these covenants against this property does come to light you can perhaps make them an offer to remove the covenant.

Generally, I don't worry too much about covenants because they are normally historic, and a previous owner will have insured against them already.

Insuring against a covenant is a one-off payment, so yourself and future owners will be afforded the same legal protections as the previous owner.

LAND REGISTRY

The land registry is a department of the government, founded in 1862, and was set up as a means to register ownership of land and property in England and Wales. Scotland has a different but somewhat similar system; the Land Register of Scotland.

All land must be registered with the Land Registry, and by this I also mean any property that is built upon it.

Every year in England and Wales HM Land Registry adds some 300,000 newly registered estates. HM Land Registry safeguards land and property ownership against **£7 trillion, and** enables £1 trillion worth of personal and commercial lending to be secured against the same property. It is worth noting here that HM Land Registry is so keen to ensure that land is correctly registered, it is the body that pay out when there has been fraud or forgery; in the year of 2017-2018 over £22 million of indemnity payments were made.

It is the responsibility of this government department to record all of the information regarding ownership and the interests that affect land and property for owners with a land title that is guaranteed by the government.

Anyone who buys, sells or takes out a charge against a property must record these with land registry.

A LEGAL CHARGE

A legal charge allows any lender to protect against the money that they have lent to an individual for a property or for land. A charge allows the mortgagee or lender to apply to sell the property if you default on your mortgage and ensures that their investment is protected. It is a legal document signed by the borrower which is registered against the property at the Land Registry and alerts any potential buyer of the existence of the debt.

So, in simple terms when you apply for a mortgage, the building society or financial institution will put a legal charge on the property on the day of purchase. This stops you from selling the property and not paying them back the money loaned by them upon completion. There were 24,672 registrations of Land Charges in 2018-2019, an increase of 3.9% against the previous year.

TITLE PLAN

This is a plan that indicates the general boundaries of the property. When talking to your solicitor you should look at the plan and ensure that you are buying what you expect.

These boundaries are normally evidenced by a red line on the plan.

LOCAL SEARCHES

These searches are carried out by the Local Authority and paid for by the purchaser. It is an investigation into the local area and lands of the property you are hoping to purchase. This is a vital part of the conveyancing process and form part of the property searches that come with buying a house or leasehold flat.

How long do these take? Anywhere from 7 days to 6 weeks, depending on the local authority, how busy they are and how many staff they use to get the searches carried out.

If you are thinking about buying a property for the first time, you will probably have heard a lot of talk about how difficult it is to buy these days. And whilst there is a new set of challenges facing first-time buyers now, successive governments have made significant efforts to help young people purchase a property and have promoted the values associated with homeownership.

I know the average age of the first-time buyer has gone up substantially since I bought my first house. However, I still believe owning property is a brilliant opportunity to gain independence and invest in your future. The government is doing its best to help, lending part of your deposit at no interest for the first five years. To qualify for this Help to Buy scheme, you must purchase a newly converted property or a newbuild house. This is due to be replaced by a Help to Buy equity loan. You can find out more from the government website to check what is currently available and for additional up-to-date information.

At the time of writing, interests rates are incredibly low, and certainly far lower than they were when I was first buying property. Additionally, where they are able to do so, parents are often quite generous when financially aiding their children onto the housing ladder. And a vast array of mortgage products means that there are a number of flexible deals that allow parents to assist.

You may believe that you can't buy in the area where you want to live. This may be true, and you may therefore need to compromise. In looking at the surrounding areas you will find that these places can often have a lot to offer themselves and have the added bonus of getting you onto the property ladder. In a later chapter I also discuss some of the alternatives to conventional home ownership; shared ownership is particularly useful if you are looking to live in a pricey area.

Purchasing your first home is an extremely exciting time. Even if it is a stretch to buy the property, it is a wonderful thing to achieve. If you think the mortgage payments are going to be hard for you to pay back, you could always rent a room out and use that money to help. At the time of writing, the government allows you to earn £7500 a year before you have to pay any tax when renting a room out in your property. You can research if this is still the case via the government website.

As a first-time buyer, you can also benefit from not paying any stamp duty (at the time of writing). This is a massive advantage over the rest of the market. Check that this is still the case by always checking on the government's website before you start to look at buying.

CHAPTER 6
TAKING THE PLUNGE

Your parents or friends may be offering advice about what to buy and where. They may even put doubts into your mind over whether now is the right time to buy your first home, or to move on to your next.

Everyone can quickly become property experts. However, these comments can be fuelled by jealousy, misinformation or their own biases based on their personal situation. Your home is deeply personal to you, so I would avoid paying too much heed to external influences.

Let's consider the worst case scenario for a moment. That is, that property prices reduce drastically.

It is true that property prices fluctuate, and go down significantly during a recession. However, it depends on whereabouts you are in the country, and to some extent the type of property you own as to how much you will be affected by this.

We must remember that the UK property market consists of thousands of micro markets, all of which have unique circumstances and qualities that dictate how each area will respond to the wider economic circumstances at play throughout the whole country.

For example, if the country is going through a period of recession, and you live near a large factory that closes down making hundreds of people redundant, this will disproportionately affect your area compared to that with a much higher rate of employment.

It is important to remember that property is a long-term investment, particularly when you consider your own personal residence. Over the last 20 years, property has inflated at a rate of approximately 5% per year. Of course, during this time there have been dips, but these generally straighten out in the long term. It is a national average and, as mentioned before, each particular area will have a unique story.

So as long as you are not looking to buy and sell the property immediately, you can be fairly confident that your home will increase in value even if there is a short-term reduction. Your home will certainly benefit you as a long-term investment.

Additionally, if you compare home ownership with renting somewhere to live, the advantages are quite clear. If you own your own home, you will be paying off a mortgage over an agreed 25-year period whilst also having somewhere to live. It is an investment in your future.

My advice here is simple. Do not let other people's opinion on what you should be doing cloud your own decision making. It is your life, and it will be your home, and you will certainly find there is a long-term benefit to owning your own property.

CHAPTER 7

WHAT HAPPENS IF YOU LOSE YOUR JOB?

If it is future financial concerns that are stopping you from getting on the property ladder, then there are a number of things that you can do should the worst happen, and you lose your job.

Of course there can be other reasons for financial difficulties, and these reasons will dictate how you deal with the issue going forwards.

For most people, their biggest asset is the property they live in. If you have equity in the property, there are a number of options available.

The first, and most obvious, is to sell the property through an estate agent if you are under financial pressure. However, please do not tell the estate agent that this is the case. They do not need to know why you're looking to sell the property, and if you do tell them, then more often than not a potential buyer will know, and it certainly will not help you achieve the best possible price for your home.

In the meantime, if you cannot pay your mortgage, you must speak to your lender immediately. Do not run up arrears without their permission. In most cases, they will be sympathetic to your situation, and will be wanting to help you because you have made the first step in sorting out your financial situation.

The most important thing to do if you do have financial problems, is not to bury your head in the sand. Most financial problems do not go away, in fact they will only get worse. I guarantee that by taking proactive steps and being positive you will feel much better.

Again, even if the situation is only temporary then talk to your lender. If you think you can start paying again in three months, then don't disappoint them. In other words, unless you are sure it's going to be three months tell them it will be four or five; that way you won't be under quite so much pressure to start paying again in three months time.

If for any reason you end up struggling to afford your monthly repayments, then it may be worth considering renting out a room, which should help you meet these payments. In the meantime, speak to your lender and continue to pay what you are able to.

PART 2

FINDING A PROPERTY

CHAPTER 8
FINDING YOUR IDEAL HOME

It is imperative that you decide what sort of property you wish to buy before you start looking for one. You should now know how much you can afford, which will help significantly in the narrowing of your likely purchase. However, you must reflect on your needs and your reason for these criteria before you begin to look.

The first reason for knowing your criteria is to narrow down your search when looking at online property portals. You'll also need the information to hand when you speak to the estate agent, who will want help narrowing down their portfolio of property to suit your needs. As well as price, you need to consider the type of property and where that property might be located. If you really don't know what you want to buy, then few people will be able to help you find out.

You may browse the windows of estate agents and property websites and therefore think you don't really need talk to them about what you are looking to buy. Yet, at a basic level, you should be able to tell them if you want to buy a house or a flat. The more specific you can be, the more helpful an estate agent can be. You want to be the first person they call when a new property comes onto their books.

When you are deciding on the location, you should buy in the best area you can afford. I was given this excellent advice years ago and I apply it to all of my developments. Even if it means you are getting a slightly smaller property, you should still look at the better area. The main reason for this is that a property in a better area will always be more desirable. The future housing market might not be buoyant but people will always look for quality when conditions are depressed. Even in a 'hot' market, property in an area of quality will still sell more quickly than in the more deprived area. There will always be exceptions to this rule, but it will work eight times out of ten.

School catchment is also incredibly important, even if you don't have children at the moment. Who knows what the future might hold! School catchment also has a positive impact on the value of a house, now and in the future. If you buy a home with the sole purpose of being within a catchment area, you need to be sure there is a place in your desired school before committing. There is nothing worse than buying property in the belief your child will go to your chosen school only to find out it is full, and you then need to pay for transport to a school that is many miles away.

If you are buying as a couple or a family, you need to have decided on your compromises before you start looking. Are you happy to accept a smaller kitchen, a tiny garden, no garage and so on? You do not want to have this argument while you are viewing the property. It is always better to get this discussion out of the way early on, as it might save you having to buy two properties when the relationship suffers under stress.

CHAPTER 9
VIEWING A HOUSE

THE FIRST VIEWING

Most people find poking around other people's homes an enjoyable experience. For the person selling the property, it's likely not to be as much fun. Remember, you might be looking to buy the house you view. Therefore, there are a few things you should do, mostly because it is good manners, but also because you don't want to upset your potential vendor.

You should always turn up on time. There is nothing more annoying for the estate agent and owner if you are not there at the right time or even the right day. Remember, the owner will have made a special effort to clean the house and to get it as perfect as possible for your visit. Don't disappoint them, especially if you want to buy the property. It will likely hinder negotiations if the owner is upset with you.

Go as an individual or couple when you first view the property. Even well-behaved children are not a suitable accessory for this initial viewing. There is no real reason for them to be there, as you are buying the property and they will only complicate this decision. Also, some owners might be delighted to see your children, but many may not. On second viewings, it is more acceptable to take the children, especially if you are seriously thinking about making an offer. Yet, I would always ask the owner's permission. Virtually all vendors will agree and asking is just about offering an appropriate level of respect; it is their home still, after all.

When viewing the property, avoid making negative comments about what you see, even if it is tempting to do so. Don't tell the seller how you are going to knock down walls, rip out the old kitchen and bathroom, or make other such thoughtless comments. These are conversations that can be had after the viewing. I have lived in my current home for 27 years. I am sure people on viewing my property might be able to see clearly how to improve my home. However, when you have lived in a property for years, you might be blind to what needs doing, and you lose a little enthusiasm for continual home improvement after so many years. There is no benefit in upsetting the owner before you begin negotiations over price.

On the other hand, do not swoon and declare how beautiful a property is either. Try to control yourself and avoid talking about how much your children would love a particular bedroom or how the dining room would be fantastic for dinner parties. You do not want to sound too keen, as it may cost you. If you have made it clear that you have fallen in love with the property, the owner may take a tougher negotiating stance. If you tell the owner that you must complete in eight weeks, it can have the same effect. Therefore, keep details about your situation to a minimum.

When viewing the property, you should always ask about the neighbours. Potentially, you won't be told the whole story, but whatever you hear will be useful to your decision-making process. Under new laws, if there is a dispute with a neighbour, the owner should declare this to you. Try to get as much information during the viewing to avoid problems with the acquisition later.

Avoid making an offer while you are still in the property. People who make an offer on impulse after first viewing the property hardly ever proceed with the sale. These buyers tend to change their mind once they have thought about it for a while. My heart sinks when someone viewing one of our properties makes an immediate offer, as I know in the end, this impulsiveness means they will rarely continue with the sale. Similarly, as is the case with most of the big decisions that we make throughout our lives, a period of reflection and consideration is always a good idea.

I am also aware that people do not make an offer on a property if they have three or more viewings. These multiple visits are a way of talking themselves out of the purchase, as they begin to see all the problems and none of the benefits. If a couple keeps coming back to see a property, it is usually because one is keener than the other and this will rarely result in a sale.

THE SECOND VIEWING

Before you go on your second viewing, write down some practical questions, it would be helpful to have answers to. You might want to see where the water meter is, the electricity meter and whether your furniture will fit in the rooms. You should also talk about the local schools, ask what they are going to leave carpets, curtains and so on and anything else that can form the basis of a commitment before you begin negotiating. Making a note of these will stop you from forgetting them in the moment.

Some other practical questions might include:

- When was the property built?
- When was the property last rewired?
- When was it last redecorated externally?
- Has there been any damp or other building problems with the property?
- How good is the broadband and mobile phone signal?
- Who is responsible for the boundaries, the owner or the neighbour?

When you first arrive, check your reaction to the property. Does it look even better than you thought before? If so, that's excellent as it is likely that this is the property for you. However, if you begin to feel some doubt, be sure to pinpoint what is causing you to feel uneasy and decide whether is it something that could be changed, otherwise you'd have to learn to live with it.

As with the solicitor, the mortgage broker and the estate agent, a successful purchasing process will be helped by a good rapport with the owners. When you are viewing the house, make sure you are pleasant and polite. I am sure you always are, but you need to make an effort to connect with these people. If they have a dog, make a fuss of the animal and mention how much you love pets. The same if they have cats – you love all cats. I am sure you get the idea.

You might worry that this is a shallow approach. However, if it saves you £10,000 when negotiating, you will see the benefit of the connection you have made. Also, building a relationship with the vendor means it will be easier to approach them later in the process if there is an issue or a deal-breaker. The rapport you build could be the difference between the deal going through or not.

Nevertheless, you shouldn't get excited and talk about how wonderful you think the house is; keep your thoughts to yourself as much as you can. You don't want to give the vendor the idea that you would do almost anything to complete the deal. Your excitement might also encourage them to conclude they are on to a good thing, and they might not move at all, and instead just apply your ideas for home improvement.

If you are offered a cup of tea, then you have succeeded in forming this rapport. Take this offer of a drink as an opportunity to ask lots of questions about their plans for the selling process. You can get an idea of how quickly they might want to sell the property. Hopefully, they'll feel so relaxed with you they'll start to tell you how desperate they are to move; how they have a new job in a different area or some other detail that hints that you can start your negotiation at a much lower price.

You should leave the property for this second time without making promises or commitments. Just let the vendor know that you want to take a bit of time to think about the house, which should be the truth.

A THIRD VIEWING?

If you really need a third viewing, and some people do, you need to be aware that you might begin to annoy the owners of the property. You could also irritate the estate agent, which might not seem so important but, as I have mentioned, you should try to be on good terms with the professionals leading the purchase process. Estate agents tend to dread the purchaser who asks for a third visit, as it usually means they will not proceed with the sale.

If you can't resist this third viewing, why not get the deal agreed and view the property after you have cemented your relationship with the seller. You could leverage the rapport you have built up from the second visit, helping you to reduce the asking price. A third visit may jeopardise this position.

My advice would be to make an offer after you have viewed it for the second time to avoid damaging any rapport you have built up. The third visit, without an offer, is usually a frosty affair and quite awkward. Generally, a seller is quite happy to accommodate a further visit after an offer has been made.

CHAPTER 10
VIEWING A PURPOSE BUILT FLAT

A flat that is designated as being purpose-built is labelled as such because it has been built to be mortgageable with banks and building societies, and have not been converted from any other type of building. It is a popular option for first-time buyers. Whereas before, such buyers aspired to a two-up-two-down terraced house with a garden, they now wish to live in a luxury flat.

When you view a flat, there are far more questions to ask, compared to viewing a house. You might think this is strange, as a house is much bigger and comes with land. However, there are a host of unique concerns you should address when considering the purchase of a flat and I want to guide you through these in some detail.

A NOTE ON GRENFELL TOWER

One of the more essential checks now is the exterior cladding installed on blocks of flats. The problem of combustible cladding became apparent after the tragedy at Grenfell Tower, which cost so many lives in London. Your first question about an apartment should be in the interest of securing your health and safety.

SOCIAL HOUSING

Firstly, you must check if this purpose-built block of flats has been designated as social housing within the development. Most councils across the UK require a developer to offer up to 33% social housing in any planning application that exceeds 1000 sq. m.   A delicate point, but one worth questioning, is the mixture of rentals and privately-owned properties close to each other. The block of flats may have primarily been purchased by a housing association who will then offer units to people who cannot afford to buy.

In my opinion, private ownership alongside housing association properties in the same building does not work. I would advise you to cancel any appointment to view a property with a mixed tenure. There are smaller blocks with no social housing or bigger blocks where the developer has negotiated a commuted payment. A commuted payment means they have given a sum of money to the local authority to invest in social housing elsewhere, separate from their development.

CONVERSIONS

Throughout my career as a property developer, most of my projects have been conversions from commercial to residential. People have been splitting and converting properties for many years. Yet, the building societies have only been keen to lend on these for the last 30 to 40 years or so. Lenders became happier to fund conversions because the more recent ones were completed with greater professionalism and full adherence to fire and building regulations.

If the conversion was completed more than 30 years ago, you should take extra care to check the building. You should be able to work this out by looking at how much time is left on the lease. Be aware that some developers have also bought and upgraded older conversions, so you may wish to ask this question too. You should find that upgrades to the conversion will bring the flat up to the required specification for fire safety and soundproofing.

The most apparent issue with a converted building is that the external fabric of the flats will likely be older than if you purchase purpose-built accommodation. Therefore, maintenance costs could be higher. This is not always the case, but it is worth asking the question. When you buy a converted property, you are likely to enjoy much bigger rooms and a property with far more character. Consequently, you will balance up any increase in maintenance costs with these benefits.

SERVICE CHARGES

You should also ask what service charge you will be expected to pay each year. This charge is an amount of money required to keep the communal internal and external areas of the block in good condition. There will typically be a management company that oversees the cleaning and maintenance and pays for any property insurance. There should also be a sinking fund, where money is stored in case there is a large job with a higher cost sometime in the future. If they do not have such a fund, you may be asked at some point in the future to make a significant one-off contribution to communal repairs.

This might seem an additional charge that you feel unwilling to pay. However, if you own a house on a freehold, you will still need to pay for the maintenance, decorating and the insurance each year. Some freeholders maximise the profits on a lease by making as much money from the management company as they can. Fortunately, the government recently brought out laws to stop freeholders doing this, and if 50% or more of the residents agree to a change in the management company, then this must happen.

The residents can then purchase the freehold from the current owners, and there is little the owner can do about it. For more information see the Leasehold Reform, Housing and Urban Development Act 1993. The current owner does have the right to take the issue to a property tribunal, where the amount of the service charge can be agreed. There is no appeals process to the decision of this tribunal, so what is decided is final.

Therefore, it is in the best interest of the current owner to keep dealings with the residents open and transparent. I believe this change in government policy has been a good thing for the property sector, as it has given buyers the confidence to buy leasehold flats.

GROUND RENT

Next, you should check the amount of ground rent you will need to pay per annum. The amount you might pay can range from £1 to more than £600 per year. Fortunately, the government's revision of property law has also helped buyers here. It has been recommended ground rent should be no more than 0.1% of the purchase price. Consequently, if you are buying a flat for £100,000, you can pay no more than £100 ground rent per annum. The only way this could rise is with inflation. This change in the law has combatted some of the exceedingly high ground rents that some housebuilders and others were charging on new properties.

I have recently developed 150 flats and adhered to this recommendation for the cost of ground rent. I believe most developers will do the same, and many financial institutions will not lend on a new property where the ground rent is set above 0.1% of the purchase price.

However, the law on ground rent is expected to undergo significant changes in the coming year, so please check government guidelines for the most up to date advice.

LEASE EXTENSIONS

You should next check the length of the lease. If it has less than 75 years to go until it runs out, your lender may not be so keen to offer you a mortgage. You need to ask whether enquiries have been made to the freeholder about the possibility that the length of the lease will be extended.

A request for an extension to a lease is becoming increasingly more common. Technically, you need to own the flat for two years before asking for this extension. However, by law, the freeholder cannot refuse you. Although, depending on the value of the flat and the length of extension requested, you could be expected to pay for these extra years.

The payment is calculated using a set formula, which accounts for the extra value to the flat due to the extension of time. Typically, the extension would be to increase to the original length of the lease. There are websites online and surveyors where you can seek information about the lease extension and its cost.

Even though the freehold owner can insist that you must own the flat for two years prior to requesting an extension of the lease, you should really make this part of your buying process. Knowing the answer to this question will speed up the process dramatically.

Again, if the leaseholder is asking for an unreasonable amount of money for the extension, you can seek a decision from the Lands Tribunal. Again, there is no right to appeal, and both freeholder and leaseholder are tied to the decision. Seeking a decision from a Lands Tribunal is not an expensive process and could save you some money.

You should also note that extending the lease will increase the value of your property. Therefore, try and incorporate this increase in your mortgage application. Considering the timescale of a purchase, this might prove difficult. However, you can make the completion of the sale subject to this, and any competent solicitor will be able to advise you on this .

TIME TO VIEW THE FLAT

I realise that I promised we would talk about viewing your potential new property. However, I have spent a lot of time telling you what to find out before you even go to look at a flat. You can look and buy without taking this advice, but you risk offering to buy somewhere that you cannot resell again in the future. You do not want to fall in love with a place and then suffer the disappointment when a host of problems arise.

Assuming you have asked all the right questions, you can then go to view the flat in the safe knowledge that the service charge isn't going to rise substantially or that the length of time on the lease is not going to stop your mortgage application from being successful.

The best agents will put all this information into the property brochure. If they don't, you must ask them for the information before you even instruct a solicitor. If you wait until you instruct your solicitor, then you will be charged for retrieving this information and reviewing it.

THE NEIGHBOURS

One of the vital questions when buying a flat is the same as when buying a house. "What are the neighbours like?" It is even more important to ask this question and to try to discern the truth when buying a flat. You will find it challenging to live in a flat where there is a considerable amount of noise and disturbance, and it can severely damage your quality of life. Your home should be somewhere where you can relax – and you must know you will enjoy your surroundings.

Remember to ask if any of the flats are rented. People who rent a unit may be less careful with the property than those who have bought their home. Think about how differently you act with a car you rent and one you buy. If the block has a lot of rental tenants, then I would advise that you seriously consider whether this is really where you want to purchase your home.

It is also worth arranging another viewing for the evening. Most properties will be different throughout the day, and agents may organise viewings at quieter times. You need to see how noisy the block gets later in the day and how much disturbance you will experience from a communal hallway.

COMMUNAL FACILITIES

Firstly, you should be clear about parking from the start. There should be enough parking spaces for the number of flats, and you may only want to consider units that come with a space attached. Communal parking areas where anyone can park can cause stress and problems. Check how many flats are in the building and how many spaces have been allocated. You should consider a lack of parking to be a serious problem.

Next, you need to ask about a communal satellite dish or whether you are permitted to put up your own. If the latter is the case, then you might end up in a block that is scattered with an abundance of such dishes. You would hope that instead, cable and internet access will be offered, but you should still check the price.

There may also be blocks committed to specific suppliers, due to intervention by the management company, so again you should ask this question. The quality of the internet may also be a problem in large blocks of flats, for instance if the building has a concrete frame and concrete floors, you may need boosters to get a good signal throughout.

In a large block there may be a concierge or caretaker. This is positive, as these people are excellent and offer additional security. You may find that the service charge is a little higher in buildings where this role is an option, but I am sure you will consider it well worth the price.

Communal gardens can also be a huge bonus, as long as you have access to them. Some blocks only offer access to individual flats – usually those on the ground floor. The additional security issues from a ground floor flat are sometimes counterbalanced by this access to the gardens. When developing my 150 units on Ipswich Waterfront, I discovered our decision to include balconies made them a far more attractive prospect, and similar developments that did not offer these were certainly less favoured.

If you wish to undertake any modernisation or structural alterations, then you will need permission from the freeholder. Any modifications you wish to make should be checked through a solicitor first. You could go ahead without this permission, but when you are selling at a later date you will be asked if any changes have been made. Moreover, you may be put in an uncomfortable position of having to seek approval retrospectively, especially if you have a sale that depends on this.

PETS

You may also want to check whether or not your lease allows for pets, or if you need to ask permission to own a pet. This could be a deal-breaker for some, so you may want to ask this first. You should also find out what pets are owned by neighbours. It could be that there is a clause in the lease that allows a freeholder to rescind permission if a pet is deemed to be troublesome. In some ways, you might want a contract that offers such tight protection of your financial interests, as you don't want things out of your control devaluing your investment.

THE MAIN MESSAGE

As you can see, there are a lot of checks to make in regard to the purchase of a flat. Many of these things will be checked by a solicitor during the purchase process. However, you might be best to find these things out before instructing a solicitor, as it will cost you a lot to find out afterwards.

Although buying a flat might sound daunting, I hope I haven't put you off your purchase. Buying a flat or apartment has become an increasingly popular option, especially in urban areas, where there are options for those looking to rise up the property ladder or those who intend to purchase a luxury penthouse.

CHAPTER 11
VACANT PROPERTIES

When I was young, my father was an estate agent. As a child, going to visit vacant houses and running from room to room was so exciting. And to my young eyes each property was enormous, more so than it really was because, without furniture, every property looks bigger. However, when vacant, all of a property's flaws are on full display.

A furnished house can hide a multitude of sins. I know that if I were ever to sell my house and to move all of the furniture out, it would look pretty shabby indeed. So, let's hope I never have to!

You need to view an empty property with these two facts in mind: it will look bigger than it is, and each and every fault will be exposed.

One benefit of a vacant property is that you can spend as much time looking around as you like, giving you a clear understanding of what needs to be repaired and modernised. You can rummage through the attic, take a careful look under the stairs, and generally spend more time inspecting the nooks and crannies than of an occupied house. Whereas if a home is occupied, the owners won't be too keen on you rifling through their fitted wardrobes.

Another benefit of a vacant property is that there is no onward chain. This makes the transaction easier, quicker and provides a lot more flexibility than being in a long property chain.

There are lots of reasons why a property might be vacant. Firstly, the current homeowners may have inherited the property. This is a good thing, as the transaction will likely be more business-like, with rational decisions on value and what they are willing to accept for the property. In fact, you may find them more accommodating with regards to a lower bid, as they want to process the estate quickly. They may want to sell the property before winter, for instance, when they would be forced to switch the heating on to protect the pipes. You may also find them wanting to move fast as insuring the property will cost them a lot more due to increased security risks.

There are also sellers who will have already moved to a new property, using a bridging loan while their former home is being sold. The good news is that a bridging loan is expensive, so they won't want to pay the interest for too long. Another reason for a vacant property is that it may have been repossessed by the lender. In such a case, this makes the transaction straightforward and rapid.

Although most of these scenarios prove to be positive, it is still essential to get to the bottom of why a property is empty. If the estate agent doesn't give you a satisfactory answer, maybe the neighbour might. There are likely to be people in the local area capable of providing you with a complete history of the property, should you choose to ask.

Yet, whatever the reason for it being empty, you are unlikely to fall foul of an owner changing their mind halfway through the transaction, which happens a lot when the home is still occupied. Also, you should be able to borrow the keys while the purchase is going through and get an estimate for work to be done. If you build a strong relationship with the estate agent, you might be able to negotiate for this work to be done between exchange of contracts and completion; and you are therefore able to move in as soon as the transaction completes.

In short, there are distinct advantages to a vacant property, as you can see precisely what you are buying with your own eyes – everything is visible. With a furnished property, you may be fooled into thinking that you are taking something on that needs little work. However, once a seller moves their furniture out of an occupied dwelling, you may find that there is a lot more to be done than you thought. Just don't be shocked when the property is eventually filled with your own furniture, and it feels so much smaller than you first thought. Always carry a tape measure!

CHAPTER 12

ISSUES ASSOCIATED WITH DIFFERENT TYPES OF PROPERTY

It is one thing to buy a property fully aware that it needs renovation, however it is quite another to buy a property, assuming that it doesn't need much maintenance or refurbishment, only to find out once you've moved in that there is a lot more to do than you previously realised. In this case, you won't have budgeted for the extra costs involved, or appreciated the inconvenience that this can cause.

There are definitely some types of property that you should be wary of, where I would recommend instructing further investigations, or even requesting a survey, particularly if there is anything on initial inspection that alerts you to potential issues.

Now, when I say survey, I'm not necessarily referring to a structural survey. For instance, there are surveys that are carried out by a damp and timber company, a roofing company or an electrical contractor; which are much cheaper and sometimes even free. A surveyor will likely suggest that you have at least some of these people out for specialist advice.

Property can be broken down into categories, and all pose distinct potential issues.

THATCHED HOUSES

It may look picturesque, or even be the perfect chocolate box cottage, but thatched houses are a little like the film Jaws; it's what's lurking beneath the surface that you need to be concerned about.

You should be aware that more often than not, these timber-framed properties have no foundations whatsoever. Instead, they have a soleplate, which can become rotten, running the full length of the property.

There are two types of thatch: the more expensive is Norfolk reed, lasting between 30 and 50 years; the second is straw and lasts up to 30 years. Many years ago I lived in a thatched cottage, and before I sold it I tidied up the ridge; the area at the top of the roof that is most exposed to the elements. By repairing the ridge, and renetting the thatch to keep birds and other creatures at bay, I was able to sell the cottage far more easily.

Thatching is a very skilled profession, and in many cases there is a waiting list of 2 years or more. However, if you get the thatcher round for a survey, you can always see if it is possible to get your name slightly further up the list.

Surveyors are also generally very cautious with regard to properties that have a history of deathwatch beetle, which can be extremely destructive, making it more challenging to get a mortgage and in some cases can be impossible to remove. Woodworm, however, will alert a surveyor's attention, but is generally far less harmful and is definitely treatable. Both of these are far more common in older houses with timber frames.

LISTED FARMHOUSES

Again, all of the concerns associated with a thatched house due to a timber frame will apply to a listed farmhouse, and as such, the timber frame and soleplate need inspecting. However, here you are likely to have a peg tiled roof. And, like thatch, peg tiled roofs are expensive to replace.

BRICK-BUILT HOUSES PRIOR TO 1900

These are normally well constructed, and houses built around this time tend to have a slate damp proof course, which are generally reliable. Houses of this era also tend to have lovely high ceilings and large sash windows. Of course, if a house is listed you will be required to retain these windows, but if it is not, I would recommend ensuring that they are in keeping with the original features of the house.

VICTORIAN TERRACED OR SEMI-DETACHED HOUSES

Most of these houses are well built, with well-proportioned rooms. A majority have slate roofs, and whilst there is nothing wrong with them, you should check that there aren't too many clips holding the roof slates together. Clips are installed to stop the slates from slipping, these tend to corrode over time, so this is a sign that the roof may need to be replaced.

HOUSES BUILT BETWEEN 1930 AND 1960

These are also often relatively well-built houses, and where they are in the country determines whether they have tiled or slate roofs. Generally speaking they have good-sized rooms and some may have the original metal Crittall windows, which will normally need replacing, although if it is a listed art-deco property, they cannot be removed.

A lot of the later properties, especially ex-council houses, may have interlocking concrete roofs. Such roofs became less common from the 1970s. The tiles are very heavy so some concrete roofs have sagged under the weight.

During this period housebuilders were getting greedier and building smaller sized houses squeezing more profit out of each plot and generally smaller gardens too. On the whole, they are not built to such a high standard, for example the doors were much cheaper and lighter. Some experimented with hot air central heating which was a complete disaster, but some still have that system now. Others experimented with ceiling heating, again, definitely not recommended!

BUNGALOWS

There aren't many bungalows built before 1900, unless you consider converted properties. However, like many modern properties they haven't been built to the same standard as the older houses.

Being only one storey high is often an advantage with regards to maintenance, particularly when it comes to accessing and making repairs to roofs and guttering. However, you may find that a lot of renovation or modernisation is needed because they tend to have been occupied by older people.

And on a value for money sidenote, whilst not having stairs is an advantage for many, you are likely to get a lot less square footage for the same price than if you were to buy a house.

FORMER COUNCIL HOUSES

These houses were well built, and certainly constructed with the intention of lasting. They are also normally of a reasonable size and come with generous gardens.

Now I will go through some common problems that can affect all types of properties.

DAMP

Those of us who are more experienced tend to be able smell damp as soon as we walk in. The most common type is rising damp. If the wallpaper is peeling off the wall towards the bottom, if there is a sign of mould or if the plaster feels damp to the touch then I cannot stress how important a damp proof survey would be.

If the property is found to have a damp proof course that has failed or no damp course at all then the contaminated plaster needs to be taken down, before injecting the wall and replastering.

Although the existing owner might say they have a damp-proof guarantee from work done some years before, and most of these are for 25 years, I've never known anyone manage to successfully pursue a claim years later. I would therefore assume that the following work will need to be done, and you should factor in these costs.

Damp-proofing is time-consuming and expensive. Do not be misled when you get the quote and think, 'Oh! This isn't too bad,' as it will probably not include the replastering of the walls. You should factor in any potential unforeseen costs, so make sure you have a firm quote for the job. You will then receive your brand new 25 year guarantee! Please make sure you will receive this and that it is from a reputable insurance company. This certificate will be more important to your lender than it is to you.

DRY AND WET ROT

This is something that people do get very worried about, and rightly so. If floorboards are bouncy when you walk across them, this is a potential sign that some of the joists are giving way below; these support the floorboards.

Dry rot is caused by fungus and is extremely serious; it can get behind plaster, destroy wood and cause serious damage.

Dry rot is dealt with by cutting out any affected wood, before replacing it with specially treated wood as well as using a fungal treatment on any neighbouring wood which is likely to fall victim to the dry rot.

Wet rot appears when there is an ingress of water and normally occurs lower in the building. Alternatively, there may have been a leak in the downpipe. Leaks can be very destructive and the affected guttering needs to be cut out and immediately replaced.

It is very important that all the guttering is checked to ensure that it is not leaking. This is an obvious cause of wet rot. The timbers affected by wet rot also need to be cut out, but you must ensure there are no more leaks, otherwise the same problem will return again.

Both wet rot and dry rot will not spread any further if they are cut out.

I have already mentioned deathwatch beetle and woodworm, and so, like with those same problems, you need to ensure that you have a report carried out by the relevant timber specialist.

Once again they will give you a 25 year guarantee but don't hold your breath as to whether if you come back in 20 years' time on a 25 year guarantee the company will still be in existence or prepared to put something right. There will be many caveats on the certificate, for instance, if the installer has not installed the product correctly in the first place as per the instructions.

We all know the challenges of relying on a warranty when you purchased a product a year ago, even when we believe we have all the requirements for our repairs or replacement, sometimes you get there and find there's something you have missed. I would always assume, and certainly until proved otherwise, that you will need to pay for any timber and damp treatment whether or not there is a current on a property.

ROOF TIMBERS

Roof timbers are certainly one element of the construction that needs checking for any sign of rot and the general strength; particularly if they have previously been treated for wet or dry rot in the past. Whilst undergoing any inspection, please check that there is a floor and plenty of insulation in the roof voids. If there isn't a lot of insulation in the loft, fortunately this is a part of the house where it is easy to spray insulation, rather than downstairs where carpets or flooring will have to be pulled up.

ROOFING

Take a look from across the road at the property and at the roof in particular. If you can identify sagging this is a sign of one of two things: either the roof tiles are too heavy for the existing roof trusses[2]; or there is dry or wet rot.

If it is an old roof, you must check that it has felt and batons underneath the tiles, most will. Again, check that it has ample roof insulation, if it doesn't then do not despair because there may be a number of grants available through the local authorities to help with the costs.

If the house is terraced or semi-detached you should ensure that there is a firewall between you and the property next door. A vast majority of these have now been installed, but if it is a very old property that someone has lived in for many years it may not have been.

TILED ROOF

There are countless different types of tiles, so for your sake, I won't go into detail on every different type. There are a few very common types. One of which is the peg tiled roof: small flat tiles which are more expensive and therefore normally on more expensive properties. Another is pantiles: these are large grooved tiles, which were originally used on farmhouses and outbuildings, but have since become far more commonplace.

Another common type of roof is slate. If you look at a slate roof and it has lot of clips, this means the roof has been repaired. Eventually these clips will corrode and break, meaning more slippage will occur.

It is also important to consider that there are a number of types of slate roof. These include natural slate, which is expensive but is also very hard wearing and requires little maintenance. There are also different options for artificial slate, which is far cheaper but does come with higher maintenance requirements.

---

2 Roof trusses form the wooden structures on top of which the tiles or slates are placed.

You'll be able to see from an external inspection whether or not there are broken tiles on the roof. If they are, this is a sign that the roof is been up a long time and that the frost probably has got into the tiles and broken them.

Depending on the general condition of the roof they can just be replaced but bear in mind that these days, that you're likely to need scaffolding, which is not cheap.

ELECTRICAL WIRING

A lot of houses will now come with an up-to-date electrical report on the property, so do always ask if there is one and be a little bit suspicious if there is not. Hopefully when you ask the question regarding when it was last rewired it will be answered honestly.

There are a few tell-tale signs such as the age of the power points and light switches and ceiling roses. If these look like they're from the 1970s or '80s then I would generally expect the property will require some updating even if it's just the light switches and the power points, so you must investigate. A lot of fires are caused by electrical faults.

BOILERS

Most houses have gas boilers, again look at the boiler and see how old you think it looks. You may find that there is a certificate on the boiler to say it is in good order. If there isn't and it looks quite old you could ask for one to be carried out. It may be that the boiler is currently working but needs replacing in a few years. At least if you have the information you can then plan for the cost of replacing it.

These days there are some electric systems called wet heating systems. Simply this means that there are radiators in the boiler that pump around hot water. Up until recently these have been very expensive to install and run. However, they are becoming more competitive in terms of price and efficiency.

UNDERFLOOR HEATING

I appreciate this is a modern phenomenon but a word of warning, under floor heating throughout the whole house can be quite expensive to run; so please check out the monthly electrical bill. Many people just put it in bathrooms and kitchens which is much more economic. However, there is definitely something appealing about having the walls free of radiators.

If you're buying a property in the countryside, it's likely to have an oil boiler. This will be due to the fact that gas is not laid in to the area. Oil boilers are more expensive to purchase and traditionally always more expensive to run than gas boilers. Hopefully your boiler will come with a certificate but do check that the tank is well positioned; not too close to the house in case of fire. The more modern plastic tank is far better than the old-fashioned metal one.

WINDOW FRAMES

A lot of people ignore the state of the windows and more importantly, the frames of those windows. If they are made of softwood, they need regular maintenance and don't last as long as hardwood. A quick way to check whether the windows are in good condition, and one used by surveyors, is to see if a car key goes into the wood. If it does, they are rotten, even if they have a fresh lick of paint over the top. Although, I must warn you that if you haven't already bought the house, the owners may be a little annoyed if you put a hole in their window frames.

Sometimes these days I consider myself to be in the wrong business. Having been Chairman of the local Conservative Association I have canvassed on many occasions and knocked on many doors, which, along with the windows, are invariably PVC these days. It always amazes me how many plastic windows and doors have been installed across the UK.

The reason of course is that they are maintenance and draught free and, on the whole, seem to last quite a long time. Any windows that appear relatively new should come with a FENSA certificate. This certifies that the windows meet building regulation standards and are energy efficient. When you purchase the property your solicitor will check that the FENSA certificate is in place and receive a copy.

DOWNPIPES AND GUTTERING

When viewing a property it is vitally important that you check that the guttering is in good order. If there is green moss on the wall where the guttering runs, it is likely that it is faulty. If necessary you can always return to the property when it is raining to assess the situation then. Guttering should be regularly checked and cleaned out, if at all possible.

In the old days guttering was wrought iron which is now very expensive to replace, but some of the aluminium guttering which a lot of people are putting up on converted barns and similar buildings is very good. Then of course, there are the plastic imitations; PVC pipes are by far the most common choice now.

The soil pipes are named as such because they take the waste from the toilet, bath and handbasins to the drains. And the downpipes take the water from the roof; please make sure neither of these are leaking, as this is a common source of damp as mentioned before.

REPOINTING

Pointing is the concrete between the bricks on the facade of the house. If the concrete is crumbling and soft, take a key and rake it gently: if it all starts coming off then you know that some, if not all the brickwork needs to be repointed. In other words cementing in between the bricks again.

This is quite a time-consuming and expensive job but could be done by a DIY enthusiast.

RENDERING

Some properties will have a render over the brick, concrete being the most common option, but it will crack after a while and will need repainting, normally once every five years, along with the rest of the property.

If there is active cracking, then that's a sign that there is movement and further investigation will be needed. It used to be that builders and property developers would render properties in concrete to hide the cracks and other problems, although this doesn't tend to happen now.

When it comes to a listed building it should ideally be rendered in limewash. It is the superior choice and more visually appealing, but it does come with a higher price tag; it is also far more difficult to apply.

GARDENS

When you're considering purchasing a property, it is essential that you know early on which fences are your responsibility and that there haven't been any disagreements between the neighbours over ownership about which one belongs to whom. Always ask such questions.

Also consider any large trees, as if there are any near to the house, their roots could potentially be spreading under the house and into the foundations, causing problems now or in the future. If the tree is on your land, then at least you are in control of the situation. If the tree is on your neighbour's property, getting them to take it down will be a lot harder.

As I mentioned before if you're in a conservation area you will need permission from the local authority to take the tree down. This doesn't mean they won't give you permission if it's causing a problem to the structure of the property; most councils will accept the fact that it needs to come down. Remember that if you don't get this, it can lead to a hefty fine.

CHAPTER 13
SUBSIDENCE

I could write a whole book on property subsidence, and whilst this book does not focus on structural problems, they have been mentioned and as such I think it is worthwhile for me to touch on the matter, if only briefly. Knowing the basics about subsidence has the potential to save you money, time and heartache. There is little point falling in love with a property, only to find out it has major structural problems. And remember, there are very few, if any, lending institutions that will lend you money on a property with structural problems.

Subsidence is caused the earth beneath a building moving or sinking. I know that this strikes fear into the heart of most, particularly when they are told the property has subsidence, has had subsidence, or is part of an insurance claim as a result of subsidence.

However, I would like to point out that if the property has not moved for many years then it will likely get a clean bill of health from a structural engineer. If this is the case, and if the property is mortgageable and insurable, then I would not be concerned about purchasing the property.

There are a few quick ways of visually telling if the house has structural problems.

CRACKED EXTERNAL WALLS

You should easily be able to see when brick walls have cracked. Sometimes, this is just a result of natural weathering, but if the brickwork has been repointed and the cracking has reoccurred, then it is definitely worth getting in touch with a structural surveyor to investigate the matter further.

CRACKED INTERNAL WALLS

The most common place for internal cracking of walls and plaster is at the point where you start to climb the stairs. This is usually in the middle of the house and the weakest point.

When viewing a property, check that the door shuts correctly and look whether the doorframe is level with the ceiling. If it is not, then this is a sign that there has been structural movement.

Floors are another tell-tale sign; if the floors are on a slope or bouncy then something may not be quite right.

Again, if the ceilings are cracked, particularly along the edges where they meet the walls, then this would indicate a problem.

I also recommend paying attention to the window frames, if they're not level both externally and internally, then alarm bells should ring.

UNDERPINNING

In days gone by, underpinning[3] was the most common way of dealing with subsidence, and if the property has been underpinned correctly, it may well come with a guarantee, and therefore there is no reason why the property can't be insured against further structural damage, and again there is no real cause for concern.

Only load-bearing walls require underpinning. The process begins in the corners and then works along the length of the walls. It requires digging underneath the current foundations, and then filling this space with reinforced concrete. The foundations of the property are made deeper and stronger to stop the cracking caused by movement.

If this work is carried out by a professional firm it will normally come with a guarantee, following twelve months of monitoring, and a clean bill of health given by a structural engineer. This means you will now be able to mortgage the property and insure against future subsidence.

Some of the most common reasons for subsidence:

1. **Cracked Drains**

   Insurance companies tend to wish to monitor the property to see how much further movement takes place following underpinning. And the most common problem with subsidence is drains. Following subsidence the drains tend to crack and leak, causing the soil around the footing

---

3 Underpinning simply means strengthening or increasing the existing foundations of a building.

to become wet. Hopefully, once the drains have been repaired, the soil will dry out and the building will once again become stable.

2. <u>Trees</u>

   If there are trees close to a building, then over time the roots may well go underneath the foundations, causing the building to crack and move. Trees can cause both subsidence and heave[4]. The solution to this is to have the tree taken down, but to leave the roots in place, otherwise you will have to deal with land heave which will cause even more problems.

3. <u>Shallow Footings</u>

   It may be that the property was originally built on very shallow footings, which are inadequate for the weight of the building that was constructed above. In this case, underpinning is really the only option.

4. <u>Soil Conditions</u>

   The type of soil that the building is on can often be a problem. One problematic example is clay soil. If there is a very dry summer the clay can shrink and cause subsidence[5]. Another example, a property which has been built on land which is unstable to begin with, for example the ground has been filled with soil brought in from elsewhere prior to construction.

MONITORING THE CRACKS

Underpinning is very expensive, and as such, if the reason can be found for the movement it is often far easier to remove the source of the damage. If we imagine that it is tree roots that are causing the movement, dealing with the tree is far easier and less expensive than making changes to the foundations. So insurance companies are inclined to remove the source and then to monitor the property for 1 to 2 years via a structural engineer.

Monitoring is done by installing 'Tell Tales', pieces of glass which are put across the cracks. If the property is moving the glass will crack, and this also allows for the size of the cracks to be reliably measured.

---

4 Heave can be thought of as the opposite of subsidence. Heave is the upwards movement of soil, which in turn causes building movement.

5 This is not to say that clay soil is unsuitable for building, just that when foundations are installed, attention must be paid to the type of soil that they are being built onto.

TIMBER FRAMED BUILDINGS

What I have written above largely refers to brick-built properties. Older timber-framed houses can be hundreds of years old and are able to move up to half an inch in a strong wind. These buildings will often have sloping floors and general movement due to their age. Rather than foundations, they will have a soleplate, which will need replacing when it is rotten, along with the timbers that connect this to ground level.

CHAPTER 14

SHARED OWNERSHIP HOUSES AND FLATS

Shared Ownership schemes are effectively a cross between buying and renting a property and are mostly aimed at first-time buyers. These schemes allow you to own a share of the property and rent the balance at a reduced rate.

Shared Ownership schemes are often used for those who may otherwise be unable to get onto the property ladder; particularly those living in very expensive parts of the country and are therefore unable to purchase a property in its entirety.

These schemes are normally run by housing associations, sometimes in partnership with the local authority.

By nature, shared ownership properties must be leasehold. Ground rent and service charges have to paid on the whole property, not the part that you own. Also, please do bear in mind that the less of the property you own, the less you will benefit from any increase in value.

There is a mechanism in place which allows you to increase your share in the property. Alternatively, you can sell your share, although many have experienced the challenges associated with selling on a property like this second hand.

Rather than trying to sell your share in the property, your best option is to use a system called 'staircasing'. In this system, you increase your share from say 25% to 75%, before purchasing the balance and ultimately owning the property outright. Then, if you wish to sell it, this can be done in the same manner as for any other freehold property.

Overall, I think that for people on a modest wage or those who are keen to get on the housing ladder in an expensive area it is an ingenious scheme and one that should receive continued support. As I mentioned earlier in the book, governments over recent years have been keen to encourage home ownership and this is just another way in which they have tried to raise its level throughout the UK.

CHAPTER 15
SELF-BUILD

The government is keen to encourage people to build their own homes, to such an extent that they offer extensive tax incentives for anyone wishing to do so. You should ask an independent financial advisor or check the government website. At the time of writing you can build your own home and claim all your VAT back. Also, currently, you do not have to pay the Community Infrastructure Levy (CIL). Usually, this payment is made on all new-build properties and is assessed on a square footage/meterage basis. The money raised goes to covering the cost of schools, roads, and other local authority amenities. Retrieving VAT costs and not paying CIL might sound attractive.

If you find the idea of self-build attractive, you may need to consider the environment. Most local authorities will push you to make environmentally friendly and carbon neutral decisions. This is not a bad thing, though it can add a lot to the costs of the project. However, eco-houses that are carbon neutral do come with generous government incentives. Also, although they cost a little more to build, the running costs on the property are much lower. Furthermore, at some point you will want to sell the property, so any design choices such as these should be desirable to potential future buyers.

NON-TRADITIONAL CONSTRUCTION

The government is keen for people to invest in non-traditional construction. As this type of construction becomes more common, I suspect some of the enhanced costs associated will come down. Non-traditional construction normally means not using brick/breezeblock.

Some lenders are looking more favourably on this type of construction than they have in the past. However, you need to check with a mortgage broker to establish who will offer mortgages and whether the interest rates are higher.

MODULAR BUILDINGS

Modular construction is a process in which the building is manufactured off-site in a controlled factory setting using the same materials and designed to the same codes as conventionally built homes, but which can normally be constructed in half the time or less. Generally speaking the building will consist of 'modules' which are delivered and then connected to one another on site.

They are generally incredibly well insulated and offer all of the modern and up-to-date technology that you would expect from any other home. The government is incredibly keen to support this type of build because of these attributes, and also because construction takes only a matter of weeks.

There are also a number of producers of modular buildings that are now focusing on trying to create eco-friendly housing in a new way, by making them recyclable, fabricating them from recycled materials, by focusing on reducing the amount of energy required compared to a conventional house. Highlighting the importance of sustainability is, of course, not unique to these types of buildings but there are certainly some very innovative producers in the market at this time.

However, there are of course some drawbacks. At present, they haven't proven to be any cheaper than traditional construction although this may change as advances are made. Poland and Slovakia, as two examples, are making excellent advances in terms of price and are far more competitive than the UK and other Western European countries.

One of the difficulties for those aspiring to own a modular building is whether it is mortgageable. This is a two-fold challenge: the first challenge being because the building is constructed in a factory and is transported to its final location it makes it incredibly difficult for a lending institution to put a legal charge on the property until it is in situ.

As mentioned before, the government are trying to encourage this type of construction and as such appreciate and understand the problems. I was recently in a meeting with the Housing Minister when this topic came up, and they are now examining the possibilities of creating a scheme where they can underwrite the value of the building to the lending institution until the building is settled in its final position. Their reason for supporting this style of building is certainly, in part, as it will help in reducing the housing shortage in the UK.

As they become more prevalent, I'm certain that they will become more acceptable to lending institutions. However, I would think that a high loan to value ratio, of 80% or more, will remain quite difficult.

The second challenge is that the UK has high standards for building regulations that cover the construction of any property; and modular homes are not exempt from this. To meet this high bar the Building Research Establishment (BRE) needs to approve the construction and grant it a 60 Life, meaning that it remains habitable for a minimum of 60 years.

If you would like more information on this or are interested in purchasing a property of this type, then you need to look for a BPS 7014 Standard for Modular Systems for Dwellings. If you go to the BRE website you will find more information, and always ask the manufacturer that they can confirm that their modular build will meet requirements and if not; find one that can.

A number of these types of manufacturers, both in the UK and abroad, have approached me and asked if I would consider partnering with them to create a development based on modular properties, rather than on a traditional new-build site. Until now I have declined for the reasons mentioned above, but also because many do not have BRE approval just yet, and therefore when it comes to actually trying to sell them it will be challenging to get the support from lending institutions.

I have previously been described as being bold in some of the decisions that I have made as a developer and like to think of myself as being keen to innovate. However, I will be waiting until the case for modular-build developments is a little more proven before I get on board.

If you are still keen on purchasing one after my cautions, I would advise you even if you pay cash for one of these very well-appointed houses, ensure that it is mortgageable through the normal channels for when you do come to sell it. Otherwise, you may find that, like a caravan, it declines in value over the forthcoming years.

ECO-FRIENDLY CONSTRUCTION

A number of people get confused between eco-friendly buildings and non-traditional construction; although the two can overlap they are distinct. Being eco-friendly often requires materials to be thoughtfully and locally sourced; for example, insulating a property using straw or using building methods that were established centuries ago. This can be combined with the most up-to-date and modern building technologies in a sustainable way, for example energy sourcing can come from ground-source heat pumps, wind turbines or solar panels.

Locally sourcing or using reclaimed materials does not always reduce build cost, as this is generally not the primary focus. The government has made it possible to obtain planning permission for these types of buildings, where planning for traditional construction may not be acceptable. Please consult with the local authority planning department or a qualified planning consultant.

Many old houses made from thatch or wattle and daub can be considered to be eco-friendly in one way or another. This is because of the materials used, rather than being particularly energy efficient.

Like all non-traditional construction, caution must be exercised when assuming that the property is mortgageable.

CHAPTER 16
BUYING A NEW HOME FROM A HOUSEBUILDER

THE PROS AND CONS OF BUYING NEW

Buying a new property is like buying a new car. Of course, everything is brand-new, which is lovely. With a home, the warranty lasts for 10 years, which will cover the main structure of the property. However, like a car, as soon as you move into the house, it becomes second-hand. Therefore, unless the market value of property rapidly increases, then you will likely experience a small loss in value for the first year or two. There are a few reasons for this. You are probably paying a slight premium to buy new, and you will have been lured in with lots of incentives to buy. For instance, you may have been offered help with the legal fees or stamp duty. Homebuilders are finding it harder to inflate the cost of the property with incentives because mortgage companies now record such financial incentives as a reduction on the price of the property.

The government's current 'Help to Buy Scheme' has enabled many to get on to the property ladder. However, this cannot be used again for the next owner, and this was likely to be the developer's target market when regenerating the area.

CAN I NEGOTIATE?

With a housebuilder, anything is possible – even with larger developers. I am sure they leave a little wiggle room in the sales price, especially if you can move quickly. Therefore, make sure you are organised before approaching the housebuilder, so if you manage to negotiate a reduced price, you are ready to start the purchase straight away.

If you are looking for a more significant discount, then you should find out when their financial half-year takes place, as well as the full year-end. At these times, they may be behind the sales targets and are likely to offer better discounts at these moments in order to sell more before the results are published. Again, to make the most of this, you must be organised and ready to begin the transaction. This is where being prepared with your solicitor and mortgage broker can make a big difference.

OFF-PLAN DEALS

A lot of property developers and housebuilders will look to sell a percentage of developments off-plan; meaning that the property is sold before they begin to work on the site. This type of purchase is popular with investors, who think they are getting between 15% and 20% discount on open market prices. Yet, these properties won't be available for 18 months, so no one can say how much the property will be worth at that point. It might be that they are getting a discount, yet it could be that they have bought at full market value; you never know. Equally, if they want to sell the property straight away, which most do, then they will be competing against the housebuilder and the other finished properties on the development – but without their attractive incentives.

If you are a property purchaser who is going to become a homeowner, you need to be willing to potentially wait 18 months to be able to move in to get the discount. You will also still need a mortgage offer, in principle at least, so you are confident you can complete the purchase when the property is ready. If you are happy with this, then you need to make sure there is a backstop date; this is a date by which time the property must be completed. If you don't get a backstop date, you can't retrieve the deposit used to secure the property.

As always, remember to check with a solicitor and get professional legal advice before proceeding. Ideally, you should know that your chosen home will be ready for occupation within 6 months, unless it suits you for it to be otherwise, for example if you are saving for the deposit.

CHAPTER 17
BUYING A LISTED PROPERTY

Listed buildings are those which are considered to have some historic or architectural significance, and have an extra layer of legal protection within the planning system to ensure that they are protected for future generations. So, if you're interested in a listed building, all of the information about why this building is important can be found publicly available on the National Heritage List for England.

The National Heritage List is a database covering all three types of listing; Grade I, Grade II* and Grade II, with Grade I being the highest listing , and meaning there will be more scrutiny and less flexibility when it comes to making alterations.

92% of all listed buildings are Grade II, and I have converted or developed a number of Grade II listed properties and have lived in another for the last 28 years, living in a Grade II* listed property prior to this. I have also converted and developed Grade II, Grade II* Grade I listed properties; however I can confidently say I don't want to do another Grade I!

Listing really means that there will be additional controls over what changes can be made to the buildings interior and exterior. And, most importantly that you will need to apply for Listed Building Consent for most types of work that may affect the special architectural or historic interest of the property.

There are some obvious things that you aren't able to do, for example installing modern windows and doors. Permission may also be required for changing the colour of the external paint, and changes to the interior of the building will require consent.

Of course, if you don't abide by these regulations, and start ripping out historical fireplaces, for example, and selling them, as some have done, you will most definitely find yourself in court and could even be imprisoned.

If you are considering purchasing one of these properties, it is important to establish whether any works have been done recently and to ensure that the owner has obtained listed building consent for these works[6].

I have been very fortunate to own and live in three listed buildings, and I do genuinely believe it is a privilege to own these homes and be a part of the special history that goes along with them, and so, I do hope this hasn't put you off purchasing one. We truly are only the custodians for these buildings, and we care for them before passing the mantle along.

---

6 If there has been work done without listed building consent then it is possible to gain retrospective consent from the Listed Building Officer at the Local Authority, but this may or may not be granted. And, if you purchase the property without consent then you may well be liable for restoring the property to its previous condition or be liable for fines.

CHAPTER 18
SEPTIC TANKS AND MACERATORS

SEPTIC TANKS

For those of us that live in the countryside where there is no mains drainage, we have relied on septic tanks in years gone by to take away waste. In 2020 the law changed and now waste water can no longer be dispersed into ditches and water courses, and so must be cleaned before being dispersed. As such, now when properties are bought and sold, they are required to have a sewage treatment system.

A septic tank is a watertight container, installed into the ground and usually made of concrete, fibreglass or polythene. It holds the waste water long enough to allow solids to settle on the bottom, forming a sludge, whilst oil and grease float to the top. They are usually emptied one to two times a year.

Due to the recent changes in the law, it is essential that, if you are considering purchasing a property that is not connected to mains drainage, you ask the age of the septic tank. If it was installed prior to 2015, it is unlikely that it will comply with the latest building regulations, and as such your lender will not lend you the money to purchase the property until a new system has been installed.

If there is a full sewage treatment system in place, then you must ensure that the outlet disperses water across the land, rather than into a ditch. If the water is being discharged into a ditch then you must change the outlet.

In my experience, the rough cost of a new system, to be purchased and installed by a professional company, is between £12,000 and £20,000.

MACERATORS

Now, whilst I am on the subject of waste, I would like to add a quick note about macerators. If it were not for regularly being asked about them, I would not include this section.

Macerators are installed where there is a lack of space, hence why they are often found in en-suite bathrooms where the water pipe has to be narrow in order to fit into the space provided. Effectively, macerators allow for a narrower pipe to be used by 'chopping up' the waste.

Macerators, particularly the older ones, can be very noisy, and not something you would want to use in the middle of the night.

CHAPTER 19
LOCATION

During the process of buying a property, most people tend to focus on the positives of an area. There is a natural inclination to exaggerate the positives, because excitement drives a preference towards a location. However, looking at an area with rose-tinted glasses is not healthy, as every region has its potential issues and problems. You need to come to the purchase of a property with this balanced mindset, being prepared to see every side of the story.

NEIGHBOURS

Why would you invest £200,000 or more of your money without checking out the neighbours? It might not be so crucial for detached properties, but for terraced houses and apartments, your neighbours are a significant part of the package.

Let's consider the potential impacts of a neighbour. Imagine your neighbour rents the property from an owner who lives far away. The tenants are noisy and challenging, and you cannot get hold of the owner to address the problem. Alternatively, you could live next to an owner-occupier who does not look after the property correctly. It could look a mess from the outside, or worse still they could have a tendency to hoard, which can create unwanted odours and even encourage vermin.

Problem neighbours can detract from the future value of any property. When you come to sell it, you will have to declare to a prospective buyer any problems you have experienced with the neighbour. More importantly, there is nothing more stressful than an ongoing dispute with a neighbour. You want to be relaxed in your home, but it is hard to do when you are in litigation with your neighbours over something that probably started relatively small and escalated.

You might think that this issue is easily spotted, as the seller must declare problems when selling the house. Yet, although they might hint at problems, they are not likely to tell you everything. Try to listen carefully to what they say, as some knowledge could be a good starting point in working out the issues with neighbours. You can then do some further research if you have an inkling of concern. For instance, the owners of the property are registered at the Land Registry. For a small price, you can find out the name of the owner of the property and then check them out on social media to get a hint about their lifestyle. Alternatively, you can do what they did in the old days and knock on the door to introduce yourself.

Remember, similar to a player with a football manager, you don't need to like them to play for them, but you do need to respect them. You will be living in each other's pockets for a while, so it is always good to be polite. And, if you can avoid the small disputes and a potentially larger issue arises, they are likely to be far more amenable.

SCHOOLS

If the house is in the catchment area of a well-respected school, the property price could rise. Therefore, even if you don't have children, you should be attentive to the reputation of the local primary and secondary schools. You will end up hoping a successful headteacher remains in post long enough for you to reap the reward in the uplift of the value of your home.

You should also check out the property at the end of the school day. If the local school is on your road or nearby, you will want to know what it is like at going home time. Schools generate a lot of traffic and a constant level of noise from the playground and sports field.

NEW DEVELOPMENTS

A new property development planned near a property could have a detrimental impact on the value of the home in the future. Alternatively, some might suggest the opposite is true, as new homes will be more expensive than a second-hand home, and your property may be more desirable to a buyer.

However, there are arguments against buying somewhere where new development is planned. The most important of these is that you will not be living in a peaceful area for a while. The new development will bring lorries, builders, noise, mud on the road, and so on. Also, the government's current

Help to Buy Scheme on new homes means that these new properties will be financially much easier to buy than yours – plus they come with a new kitchen, bathroom, and carpets. The effect? It can create a two-tier market in your area, with the latest properties winning out.

NOISE

You must drive around the area close to your potential home at night, as well as during rush hours. You need to appreciate the level of noise caused by travel and by your neighbours. You should also work out where the nearest train line is to your property, as well as the closest main road.

One consideration you might not think about is commercial dog kennels. Whereas you might be able to get used to the sound of a train or road-noise, you will never tune out constant barking, especially at night.

FLOODING

You would be amazed at how few people check flood risk before instructing a solicitor. Checking such an essential detail too late in the process could cost you dearly in fees and result in an aborted house buying process. You will likely think long and hard about buying in a flood zone, especially if there will be difficulty getting insurance. Even if you can get a mortgage on the property, you are likely to have problems selling it in the future.

There are three levels of flood zone, numbered one to three, zone three being the most severe. It is unlikely that a developer would be allowed to build a home in such a zone, but you should still make sure you are not placing an offer on a house that is in zone three. Always ask the relevant question when viewing the property, and when the owners tell you they have never had a flood do not accept this answer as being good enough to suggest that the property is not at risk. Whilst many properties sit in a flood zone, they have never yet flooded. To discover the situation you should look to Environmental Agency and local flood authorities.

SOCIAL HOUSING

If you are looking to buy your first property, it tells me you are aspirational and ambitious. You want to get on in life and eventually pass your assets on to your family in the future.

There are many excellent tenants of social housing around the country, and the housing associations that provide such properties do an excellent job. However, we all know an example of a tenant who can be challenging to live close to. You may want to be sure of the mix of tenure in your area. Although most social housing is well-managed and you are unlikely to distinguish any difference, its presence in the vicinity of your property could impact on its value.

THE SHORT CUT (A RAT RUN?)

There is nothing worse than living on a road that, between seven and nine in the morning and four and six in the afternoon, becomes a rat run. People seeking a short cut nip down your street can create a mass of traffic. Checking for the patterns of transport should be a priority; though, with one million people added to the population of the UK every three years, the problem is unlikely to get any better.

PROXIMITY TO A RAILWAY LINE

It is quite remarkable that anyone would want to purchase a property next to a railway line, with trains trundling past all the time. I can only assume that they are very committed to trainspotting. However, you must appreciate that just because some people like trains, most do not want them so near to their home, and it makes it far more difficult to sell.

I understand that when you live with noise, you do get used to it, however I'm not so sure you can get past the vibration that goes through the property every time a truck or a train trundles past your front or back door.

And, whilst I am on the subject, if the seller tells you there aren't many trains please look at the timetable. I would always be wary of taking the owner's word for things and instead do your own research.

NEAR TO AIRPORTS

I recall going to look at a property near Gatwick to convert into 10 flats. The property seemed very cheap. I got inside, had a good viewing, and came out relatively confident that I could sell those properties to people working in the aviation industry. Then, all of a sudden, a massive shadow came over and a Boeing 747 came into view over the roof and it seemed close enough that you could reach up and touch it!

If you're looking to buy a property close to the airport, please make sure that it isn't on the flight path. If the property is not, it may be a very good purchase, if it is, then it will likely be blighted. This means if you put the house on the market in the future, you will get a lot of interest, and a lot of viewings, but the interest may go no further.

DOG KENNELS

This is not an obvious consideration. However, noise travels far more at night than during the day. Hence why it is so difficult to get planning permission for a dog kennel business from the local authority.

Can you imagine all that barking all day and all night? I think I could put up with the dogs being walked, but not the constant howls and whines. So, I would recommending having a quick check on the planning portal of the relevant local authority.

TRANSPORT YARD

This may seem obvious, but I advise scouting out that there is no haulage business in the vicinity of the property you wish to purchase. These businesses start very early in the morning. And, as I own a transport yard, I can tell you that there are constant complaints from the neighbouring houses.

Of course, you can go to the local authority and complain about the noise to the noise abatement officer, and they will duly come out and check the level of noise. But I ask you, why would you want to go down this route if you don't need to?

A BUSY ROAD

Whilst I do appreciate that you may want to live on a road that has great access to the motorway or dual carriageway, not everyone will think the same as you. Also, with more cars on the roads year on year, the road noise will only increase and the road will always get busier.

I live about a mile from a dual carriageway, and it is true, you do get used to the road noise and traffic. However, I'm just about far away that I have the benefit of great access and only have to put up with a little bit of noise if the wind is blowing in a certain direction.

That was clearly the view that I took when I purchased the house, balancing up the potential noise with the accessibility and convenience, deciding it was worth putting up with a small amount of noise in the end.

A SHARP BEND

This one might sound very petty, however it can be very annoying when it's dark and every time a car comes around the bend, headlights peeking between the curtains and straight into your living room in the evening or bedroom at night.

This will quickly become hugely annoying, particularly if you are a light sleeper. Also, it is worth taking into account that people will likely be changing speed and gears before and after the bend, causing extra noise.

Of course, similarly to being on a busy road, just because you don't have pets, this doesn't mean any future prospective buyers don't and a sharp bend will certainly put them off. It is worth remembering that 44% of UK households have a pet, mostly cats and dogs.

TRAFFIC LIGHTS

The biggest problem with living close to traffic lights is the sound cars speeding up, slowing down and sitting stationary with the engines running. And whilst some cars automatically stop when stationary, they also need to start up again when they need to move. For those of you that have electric cars, I accept that it is much less of a problem, and it will certainly be better for homeowners near traffic lights in the coming years.

Another issue is that you have to remember is light pollution, it makes no difference during the day, but at night when everything is dark your house may be illuminated by the glowing of red, amber and green.

WASTE DISPOSAL SITES AND SCRAP METAL YARDS

Unless you work at either one of these two places, there is little to desire to live near either. If for no other reason than the volume of lorry traffic going to and from these sites daily.

A few years ago, I purchased a Grade II listed pub and coach house. I did exactly what I hope you would do, which is to speak to the council and find out how long the site's licence had left on it and the likelihood of it being extended. I was told that it only had two more years until the site would be full, and as such the licence would not be extended.

On the basis of this, I purchased the buildings next door. To my horror, I then found out that soon after my investigations they put in an application to use the site, not for housing as I hoped, but rather as a waste transfer centre.

To cut a long story short, I sold the coach houses well but struggled to sell the converted pub, eventually negotiating a deal with the waste transfer company for them to purchase it. They were, no doubt, thinking that they didn't wish to have further objections to any future planning applications from neighbours.

I did make some money out of the deal, but not as much as I initially anticipated, so I would recommend exercising caution when considering purchasing near to any similar sites.

Scrap metal yards are much the same. I hear many stories of how these sites will be redeveloped for houses. However, in my experience very few truly are, the reason being the contamination of the land. It is very expensive to clear the site and to obtain the planning permission. As planning is so difficult to get for an alternative site, scrap metal yards are actually very valuable in their own right and probably more so than land for housing.

So, as with most things, if the owner says to you, "Oh, don't worry it's only there for another two years", definitely make your own enquiries, and really consider whether you are prepared to take that risk. I certainly won't be buying another site next to a waste disposal site or scrap yard.

NEXT TO PRISONS AND CORRECTIONAL INSTITUTIONS

Personal experience tells me that even if you don't mind, not everyone will enjoy live next-door to or near to one of these facilities.

Once again, this comes from personal experience; a few years ago I purchased a block of ten flats in Shepton Mallet. I went to view the property, thinking it was great value for money, whilst there I noticed a very interesting looking building next door.

Knowing that I had driven four hours to look at this property, the estate agent plucked up the courage to tell me that next door was a high security prison. The next thing he said to me, "The great thing is that you never need to lock your door, there are security cameras everywhere and it's probably one of the safest places to live!"

And he certainly had a point, crime was very low in the area and breakouts were very few; and if a prisoner did manage to break out, I doubt they would want to stick around.

Although, for a lot of people the thought of living next door to violent criminals would probably put them off purchasing, even if it doesn't bother you. Of course, there is the benefit of it being handy for visitation should you have a relative staying there at Her Majesty's pleasure.

Anyway, I'm sure you're wondering why I bought these flats, which I subsequently sold on at a good profit. It is simple: it was a good investment, with great rental return. In this instance, my judgement appears to have been right.

Arguably, open prisons are more of a problem to live near to rather than high security prisons. Prisoners are allowed out at weekends and sometimes during the week to work locally, and there are a lot more break outs as some prisoners don't return after being allowed out. However, they would be unlikely to hide in your garden shed for long!

SPORTING AND MUSIC VENUES

Just because you are a massive fan of a particular football team, or like going to see live music, this doesn't mean everyone else is the same. These areas will be very busy when there is an event on. Although the reverse may also be true, it may be quiet most of the time but lack parking on event or match days.

But, why take the risk? Potential buyers in the future may not think the same as you. Additionally, these venues could be shared with other organisations and become twice as busy.

<u>BEING NEAR WATER</u>

I certainly appreciate the attraction of being close to water, and in some circumstances it can also significantly inflate the price that you can expect to pay, or attain, for a property. For example, if you are overlooking a marina this can add up to 40% on to the value of your home, compared to a similar property without such views. And the same can be said for properties that overlook the sea or a river.

However, it's important to remember the cloud that may come along with the silver lining, and this is particularly important with ocean facing properties. They look great in the summer, but are cold and damp in the winter. Additionally, the salty air can cause a number of maintenance issues, not to mention the near constant window cleaning.

I personally live in a moated house, and whilst I think this to be quite attractive, there will certainly be challenges with water being so close to the house, not to mention the safety concerns if you have small children.

So, when you are looking at beautiful homes near water on the internet, it is worth bearing in mind that there is usually a downside to go along with the upside. This can come in the form of damp, flooding or subsidence.

When viewing such properties, always check how often they flood, and what steps there are to avoid this happening. For example, one of the steps I have taken, for when the water level gets too high in the moat next to my home has been to have a pump that takes the water into a deeper moat further away from the house.

So, it is worth considering, firstly what potential problems may arise from the nearby body of water? And secondly, are there reasonable steps that can be taken to mitigate the potential risks?

TIME TO RETHINK?

You are reading my book, so naturally I'm sure you are quite intelligent and make excellent decisions. And as such, I'm sure I don't need to give you anymore examples than I already have.

If a property has an issue that will likely affect the price or the length of time that it will take to sell in the future, this is probably a risk that you do not need to take.

As you can see by some of my previous examples, I have bought properties with these "issues". However, it is worth noting that I have bought and sold almost 4000 properties, and therefore have the benefit of experience. So, it is certainly worth taking a second look at whether this is a risk you are willing, and able to take. You must be sure that you can deal with any problems that may arise.

I have mentioned a few times that you should aim to make your job as easy as possible when looking to sell the property on in the years to come. Why take the risk that the property won't grow in value as much as other properties that you could have purchased? Why take the risk of constant problems during the time that you do own it?

This is particularly pertinent when you are purchasing your own home; it should be a place that you are able to enjoy and relax in, not somewhere that causes you constant stress.

Although I appreciate that this is a judgement call and you should certainly use yours. You can, of course, get a lot more for your money if you're willing to take on a property in a less attractive position. However, you should weigh this up against the potential resale issues and the growth in value of the property during your years of ownership.

CHAPTER 20
UPSIZING

Moving up the property ladder to a bigger and more expensive property is a very exciting time. It also says a number of things about you. It tells me that you are ambitious, aspirational and you are doing better financially than you were when you last purchased a property. It could be that you need more space as your family expands!

Whatever the reason, it is a really positive time in anybody's life. Now, the really clever thing to do is to try and jump an extra rung up that metaphorical ladder. Most people start off with a terraced house or a small flat, before moving up to a three-bedroom semi-detached house, before aspiring to own a detached house.

Now, consider if you could move from a terraced house into a detached house, even if it is a financial stretch. What are the advantages? Well the first being that you won't need to read my book again in a few years' time! But more importantly, you can save yourself the hassle and expense of selling and buying another property.

There are, of course, other advantages. You can better plan your life, knowing that you are going to be staying put for many years to come. Hopefully if you stretch yourself, and have a larger mortgage sooner you will be able to finish paying a mortgage several years sooner.

As I have mentioned before, property prices have increased approximately 5% per annum over the last 20 years. However, as I have also stated, in the UK property is made up of micro markets, but if we take this percentage as an average, a more expensive property is likely to increase in value more pro rata than a cheaper one.

Now, I can expect that one or two of you are questioning whether you should purchase a bigger property in a market that is difficult or where property prices are reducing? My attitude and advice is that if you already own a property, it doesn't really matter what happens in the wider market. In fact, one of the best times to buy a larger property is in a depressed market, as you will get a bigger reduction on that property.

I have a property career spanning over four decades, and I have made more money coming in and out of a recession than at any other time. So, I would of course recommend that if you are in the position to take advantage of the market, then please ensure that you do so.

CHAPTER 21
DOWNSIZING

Downsizing is a popular word these days and is mainly associated with older people who are looking to reduce the size of their property or their outgoings. The hope is that downsizing will put some money in the bank; maybe for retirement, having purchased a much smaller property. It is a good strategy for the property market too, otherwise there would be a shortage of large, family houses available for younger families to move into.

If you are looking to downsize, there are one or two things that you really need to check to make sure you are happy with your choice.

Firstly, are you responding to pressure? Quite often there is pressure from the younger members of the family for parents to downsize, sometimes to provide children with the deposit for their own properties. Alternatively, they may want mum and dad to be closer to their grandchildren. This might feel like a powerful draw, although you might end up looking after the children and working harder than before!

Rather than stray into family issues, I will stick with property.

The term downsizing clearly means you are reducing the size of the property that you are looking to purchase, which means if you have a lot of furniture, it is unlikely to fit into the new house. Getting rid of possessions you have had for a long time can be difficult. Remember, the room sizes will also be significantly smaller in your new property.

When you are looking to downsize, you many also want to benefit from closer amenities. For instance, you may hope for a local shop nearby and the property to be on the bus route. You may want to be closer to the pharmacy or the doctors. What you don't want to end up doing is moving to an area where the facilities are no better than you currently have. You may end up feeling unhappy and experience the costs of moving again.

If you are looking to downsize, first make sure it is your own decision and not your family's. Then, make sure you know what you want from the move and what you hope to achieve. For instance, do you want a small house with a big garden? Are you happy to live in a semi-detached or townhouse, even though you may have spent years in a detached property rural property?

ASSISTED LIVING

I am currently selling a site to one of the UK's large retirement developers. It is interesting to see how they operate. These developments are often referred to as sheltered housing accommodation – a smarter name is assisted living.

These developments are customarily limited to occupiers over 55 years old. However, I understand if you have a younger partner, they too can live there. Of course, most people who move into assisted living accommodation are much older than this. It is likely they downsized a few years earlier and are now looking to live somewhere where there is a warden on site.

The move to assisted living is more often than not instigated by younger members of the family. They want parents or grandparents to move into this type of accommodation to ensure they are safe and secure, with 24-hour assistance. Some developments will have a care home next door or be connected to a doctors' surgery, which might be useful in the future, if not slightly depressing.

If you think managing furniture and valuable possessions is challenging when downsizing, I can assure you it is even harder when moving into assisted living. There are benefits to the communal lounge and accommodation for visitors. Also, there is a strong sense of community, with the offer of social events during the day and in the evenings. Additionally, there are a number of levels of assisted living, with most allowing for the change in care needs over time.

However, there are drawbacks. Firstly, they are about 30% more expensive than a stand alone flat or bungalow of a similar size; though they obviously offer different features. The other drawback is that it can be challenging to get as much back on the property as you paid. You will likely pay a significant service charge tied in with the accommodation, and there are management costs for the upkeep of the structure and the facilities.

Yet, I think a lot of people take the view that there comes a time in their lives when paying out more is worthwhile. Money is no longer a primary motivator. If they are looking to move into assisted living, it is likely that it will be the beneficiaries that will be left with the responsibility of selling to the next owner.

CHAPTER 22
KNOCK IT DOWN AND START AGAIN

You may well go to view a property and find that it is in deplorable condition. The advice you are given, or the conclusion you reach yourself, is that the property needs to be demolished, and you need to start from scratch. It can be cheaper to start again in many cases, and you end up getting the home you want, to your specification. There is no need to compromise all the time. Whereas you would have to on the basis of the demands of an existing property.

If this is something you want to consider, make sure that the local planning authority will accept that the property is going to be knocked down and another property erected. For this, you will definitely need an architect, as well as a building surveyor. It is best to use an architect who knows the area and maybe one who has a relationship with people in the planning department. You want to speak to this architect about whether your hoped-for project is feasible or not.

The sort of buildings that most commonly end up being knocked down and replaced are often bungalows or small houses on a larger plot. This demolition allows you to build a more significant property and maximise the land. If it is a larger site, there may be space for more than one house.

However, we are now straying into property development, something I cover more in my other books. However, the most significant point to raise is that you have sought confirmation granting you permission to carry out your plans, before purchasing the property. Unless you have got deep pockets, please don't gamble on this; make sure first.

The only safe way is to buy the property is subject to planning permission. This process will take up to 6 months, and it may be that the owners will demand a non-returnable deposit from you. This deposit allows you the time necessary to obtain the planning permission. Even if the money is non-returnable, it is still a better option than buying a property only to find out later that planning permission has not yet been granted – that cost could be hard to recover from.

The other issue, of course, is that anybody then buying this property from you will know they cannot get planning permission. This will, I have no doubt, reduce the value of the property as you purchased it on the basis that planning could be obtained and the seller added some 'hope' to the price. In other words, you increased your offer because you were projecting profit on planning permission being granted, where the value would be added with a new building.

Even with my 40 years of property experience, having done hundreds of deals, I don't like buying a site without knowing I can definitely get planning on it. There is a relatively new system where the local planning officer has approximately 40 days to respond to your enquiry[7]. You can put in a rough plan of what you wish to achieve, and they will say yes or no within this time limit. This is a pre-application, and I would advise anyone purchasing a potential development site to do this.

Bear in mind that the response written by this planning officer is a personal opinion and not necessarily that shared by the local authority. Therefore, you still need to put in a planning application and go through the full process. This process can take approximately three months from when the application is submitted to being finally accepted by the council. In short, you really need to factor in six months to ensure you can obtain the appropriate permission on your site.

---

7 This is planning pre-application and can be useful as the planning officer will often give you advice to give you the best chances of having your planning permission granted. The cost of this will vary depending on the size of the proposed project.

CHAPTER 23
PROPERTY IN NEED OF RENOVATION

I look at a property in need of a renovation differently from those requiring an extension. The property needing an extension comes with an easily calculated building cost. You will know exactly how much you are going to spend per square footage/meterage of the new extension. On the other hand, a renovation is much harder to assess, and you are basically taking a wild guess at the costs. It will depend on precisely what you want to do and how far along the path of renovation you go.

One big question when considering renovation is whether you will live in the property while you undertake the work. With an extension, this is not an issue. It is not necessary to knock through to the extension until it is ready, making it easy to live in comfort in the rest of the property. This is not the case with a renovation. People get excited about the project and strip out the property, making it totally uninhabitable within a day. However, they have not realised how long it will likely take to put it back together again.

You must get professional advice before making a purchase of such a property. Only those who are professional builders or experienced DIY enthusiasts should purchase a house without someone with the right level of expertise estimating the work required.

If you are serious about proceeding, you will first need to speak to a building surveyor. You will likely need to understand planning permissions and building regulations, so this is an excellent place to start. A surveyor will also advise you on the approximate cost of the work and provide a full schedule, which will allow building companies to submit tenders to complete the project. Using a building surveyor will give you fixed plans to work from.

I understand that this is an additional cost, but getting the builder to view the house and assess the job can result in varying plans and costs. This makes it far easier for you to compare different builders' tenders, and will likely save you money later on.

During the viewing of the property, there is nothing wrong with inviting a builder around to give you a quick estimate of what it might cost. All you need here is a ballpark figure. Yet, if you choose to proceed, you should do so with the estimation offered by a building surveyor. Although you will not put it out to tender at this point, the estimates will help you to fulfil any requirement for information from the lender. I would recommend allowing for 20% above the estimates for unforeseen problems, or changes to the plans.

This is a time when you might want to ask for delayed completion. Under normal circumstances, you exchange contracts and are expected to complete in a month; however, if you agree a delayed completion, you can complete the tender process. By doing this, you will be ready to get cracking on the work with your chosen builder the moment you have the keys. This will save you some time between the purchase of the property and moving into your refurbished home.

Some notes about dealing with builders during renovations. Firstly, don't change your mind about the project halfway through. Builders love the opportunity to charge you a lot more money, and you are unlikely to get someone else to do this work while they are still there. You also give them the perfect reason to miss the work completion date. Secondly, allow a bit longer for the job and help the builder to get it right. You might be impatient, but if you rush into construction work and change your mind, it can be costly and disheartening.

WHERE TO LIVE WHILST THE WORK IS UNDERWAY

Your first option is to live in the property while the work is being done. This is a tricky thing to do, especially if you are a couple, as it can cause a lot of arguments and stress. Someone recently said to me that buying a home to renovate together is 'so romantic'. I put them right, as there is not much that's romantic about living without hot water or in a house without heat or plaster on the walls; and let's not even consider life without a kitchen.

If you are going to live in the property, then I always advise getting the upstairs cleaned and decorated, with a temporary kitchen and bathroom at the start of the project. You can then live upstairs while downstairs work is underway. Once the work is complete downstairs, then the builders can move upstairs to put in the finishing touches.

Alternatively, you can move into a mobile home on your site or at a caravan park. You and your children, if you have them, will find this exciting for the first two weeks. However, after this early optimism, you can take it from me that you will feel stressed living in such close proximity. It can really put a lot of strain on a relationship, and is something I wouldn't advise.

There is always a chance that the building works could take much longer than you think, and any delay will put you under pressure. If you live on site, you won't get much privacy and will take responsibility for receiving deliveries and will be on hand for constant chats with the builder. I have been thanked many times for this advice, which I also gave in my book on developing and investing for newcomers. I think I might have saved a few relationships.

The better option by far is to rent a property close by. If you think the building work will take six months, then you should take out a nine-month lease. You should take a conservative approach to timing when you are signing the tenancy agreement for your temporary accommodation.

You may worry that the cost of renting a house or a mobile home is an unnecessary expense. You might think it is better to go live rent-free with your parents. However, although parents are wonderful, this can be a stressful option. You don't want to get into a situation where Mum and Dad start counting down the days to the six-month completion date. Even if you and your parents are happy, you partner will likely not be. It is better to reduce this stress and rent a property. To help with your mindset, add the cost of the rent onto the building costs.

If you are renting, you are going to have to be confident of your finances too. Remember, for the time you are in the temporary accommodation, you will be paying both rent and your mortgage. It will be worth it though.

CHAPTER 24

RETAINING YOUR EXISTING PROPERTY

You may be in the fortunate position of owning your current property and being able to consider the purchase of another one, whilst retaining your existing home. Some five million people in the UK have already done so. To be sure of making it work, you need a reasonable balance of equity in your current property, which will secure the costs of the new purchase.

If you have 50% equity in your property, you still owe half the money on the current property. However, with the other 50%, you may be able to purchase a second property.

This is a time when your long search for the best mortgage broker will pay off. A highly rated mortgage broker should be able to search the market for a new product, a buy-to-let mortgage, which is required if you want to then rent the additional property out. More than two and a half million people have taken out buy-to-let mortgages in the last 10 years.

When the broker presents these products to you, it may be that the interest rates are slightly higher than your current mortgage. The general theory Is that you should get 150% in rent on your monthly mortgage payment. In other words, if your mortgage is £500 on the house, then the rent should stand at £750.

You might think this is over-cautious, but I believe it is a sensible and safe way forward. Remember, if you rent the property, you will also have repairs, and you will need to pay for insurance. Also, there may be the odd time when no one is renting your property, but even though the house is vacant, you will still need to make payments on your mortgage.

This second property is unlikely to be as big or expensive as your current property, especially if you are using the current equity in your retained property. Also, for tax purposes, you will have to nominate which house you plan to live in. The one you are renting out will then be subject to tax if you sell it and there is an increase in value. Only your primary residence is tax-free, the other property will be subject to Capital Gains Tax.[8] You should seek advice from an independent financial advisor on issues relating to tax, as laws are always subject to change. You might also want to ask about tax benefits or the amount of unearned income you can receive before paying tax.

On the plus side, you won't be selling a property, so you are in an excellent position to purchase another one quickly. You are not in a chain. This can lead to you getting a better deal on the new house you are seeking to purchase, as you offer the opportunity for a smoother and quicker transaction. All you then have to worry about is finding a tenant and getting the finance in place.

---

8 It is also important to remember that income generated by renting out a second property will be subject to tax.

CHAPTER 25
CONSERVATION AREAS

It is always worth checking for yourself, before viewing a property, whether it is in a conservation area. Conservation areas were created by the Listed Building and Conservation Areas Act in 1990 and were aimed at controlling specific urban areas that are of historical or architectural importance. Thus, they tend to be mostly urban rather than rural.

When purchasing a property in a conservation area, you can have a greater level of confidence that things will not drastically change in the future. This is because it is far more difficult to obtain planning permission for any new developments in a conservation area. And then, even if planning is obtained, the buildings will have to be of a specific architectural quality. Furthermore, if you wish to demolish any buildings, this requires permission.

Property prices tend to be higher in conservation areas than in a comparable locality, not just because of the protection but also for whatever reason the area was designated a protected area in the first place. It is likely the area carries a lot of architectural merit and historical importance.

Another restriction in conservation areas is the taking down of trees without the permission of the council, this is with or without a tree protection order. I was fined many years ago when I took down a cherry tree, not knowing that it was in a conservation area and that I needed permission first to do so. This was 20-years or so ago, and even then, I could have been fined £20,000. Luckily, the judge believed my explanation that I did not appreciate that one needed consent, and only fined me £2000. I had already replanted another tree.

Please, do not make the same mistake as I did. I am sure the fines are much greater these days, especially with the sensitivity to trees being cut down.

All of this should give you some confidence when purchasing in a conservation area. You can feel confident that it has been designated in such a way that it will not change dramatically. Consequently, property prices are likely to remain higher than in other areas that are close by.

A NOTE ON TREE PROTECTION ORDERS (TPO)

Having mentioned a tree protection order, it is worth exploring this in some detail. It is essential that you know if there are protected trees in the grounds of a property that you wish to purchase. If a tree does have a protection order on it, it is almost impossible to have it taken down. Therefore, if such a tree overshadows your garden, especially as it grows bigger, you need to be aware that your options are limited. If the branches need pruning, whilst you will still require permission as the branches are also protected, this is rarely withheld; uncovering more of your property and allowing for more light.

The law covers specific trees as well as areas of woodland from damage and destruction. Check with the local authority or contact a specialist person who is qualified in tree management to advise you.

If the tree needs pruning, and most do as part of good (tree) husbandry, then permission from the local authority will likely not be denied. This, at least, will give you the option of uncovering more of your property and allowing more light in.

If you want the tree removed, there are only a couple of reasons when there is a TPO. One is if the tree is close to the property and the roots may be growing under the foundation, threatening structural damage. If that was to happen, you must go to an expert and seek their opinion. You will likely still need to commit to replacing the tree.

The other reason for taking the tree down is a disease. Sadly, this is becoming quite common. Some old-school property developers used to say that if you hammer a copper nail into a tree, it will die. I can't say if that was just rumour or a genuine reason for a tree to die; either way, it is not something to get involved in. Any attempt to take down a protected tree without permission of the local authority is considered a criminal offence. It could lead to a significant fine and potentially a prison sentence.

PART 3

PURCHASING THE PROPERTY

CHAPTER 26
MAKING AN OFFER

People who are not in business can sometimes feel uneasy when talking about money. Other than making offers on a property, it is unlikely that you will have ever dealt in such vast sums before. Therefore, I can understand why some people look at this money as if it is not real. As most of the funds will come from the lender, you are unlikely ever to see or touch the cash – and maybe not even have to write the cheque, as all money is dealt with via solicitors.

However, let me assure you that the money you are offering is real. Therefore, if you can save £500, £10,000 or maybe even £100,000 on the purchase, then it means you are borrowing less money and paying less interest on your loan. Your monthly repayments will be lower, and you might be able to pay the loan off more quickly. If you are making a cash purchase, then it is even more important to get a good deal. Imagine the holiday or car you could buy with the money you will have saved.

Even if you think the property is priced fairly, most owners expect an offer below the asking price. Although, it is worth noting that the 'offers in excess of' strategy is becoming more popular, and in this case the owner could be offended when someone does offer below the asking price; equally they may consider a lower offer.

The estate agent has also probably mentally prepared their client to consider a lower offer during negotiation. Therefore, it is essential to get to know the owner and their circumstance, in order to find all the reasons why they might accept a lower offer. The best negotiation is one where both parties are happy with the outcome.

Furthermore, when preparing to negotiate remember to 'keep your powder dry'. In other words, do not make an offer unless you are in a position to proceed immediately, for example unless you have sold your own home, or if you do not have a mortgage agreed in principle. By making the offer so eagerly, you are letting the owner know just how keen you are and weaken your negotiating position. You can convey to an estate agent that you are interested without placing a formal offer.

When you are ready to proceed, you should inform the agent that unfortunately you cannot pay the full asking price for the property. There is no need to tell them why. You may have a few properties you are interested in, and it is a toss-up between the one you are talking about and these others, all held by different agents. I would not ask if they are open to negotiation, as this can sound weak.

Do not tell the agent that you think the property is overpriced: whilst it may well be, you want this person on your side. Allow them to come some way towards you, rather than alienating them by telling them they are wrong. If you take this positive approach, the agent will reveal the price reduction they think the owner will take for the property. If you hear that the owner is in no rush and has yet to find somewhere else to live, there is no point continuing with the negotiation.

Once you are confident the agent will reduce the price, you'll already have negotiated a reduction without making a commitment yourself. You need to try to get a lower offer from them first, before seeking to show your hand with your counteroffer. This counteroffer should not be your best offer, nor should it be at the top of your budget. However, do not go so low that it embarrasses the agent and annoys the owner. You will likely get no further with this negotiation.

Once you have made your offer imply that this is your best offer. The agent might not believe you, but the client might. What you are looking for is a further reduction on what they have said they will take. They may come back seeking an offer higher than the one you made, but this is fine because you will not have offered your best price at this point.

Do not get sucked into telling the agent what you could really pay for the property. Many agents are skilled at getting you to reveal this amount, but you must keep it to yourself. The person you are talking to might be acting as the bridge between you and the owner, but remember they are being paid by their client, the seller.

When they counteroffer, you should now split the difference between the two offers. It looks as if you are trying to be fair and to seek a compromise. It also gives the agent the best chance of getting agreement from their client.

It is likely that agreeing to split the difference will conclude the negotiation. However, if there are things about the property that you want to be added, extras such as the cooker, carpets, curtains, and so on, then this is the time to try to get them included.

When the negotiation is agreed, do not commit to a timescale you cannot meet. If you do, you will annoy and frustrate the owner and the estate agent to such an extent that they could pull out and find a different buyer.

For example, if they want the transaction completed within 28 days, and you know this is unachievable you need to make it clear that you think this will be difficult or indeed, impossible. It is far better to tell them now and counteroffer with a realistic time frame. However, do make such an offer subject to a timescale starting from the receipt of the sales contract at your solicitor's office. I can assure you it's extremely unusual that these timescales are absolutely adhered to in a normal domestic sale and purchase, so please don't get too caught up with timescales at this stage, nor should you pull out of a sale because you feel they are too onerous, as the sale may not actually happen at the time requested by the vendor.

So, how would this process play out in figures? Let's take a property on the market for £425,000.

- The original asking price is £425,000
- Confirmation that seller would accept £400,000
- You counteroffer £375,000
- They come back with an price of £390,000
- You suggest splitting the difference at £382,500
- They counter again with £385,000
- Again, you offer to split the difference at £383,750 and they agree.

You could be unlucky and find a seller who is unwilling to reduce the price or point-blank refuses an offer. If this is the case, make an offer you think is reasonable and leave the negotiation for a few weeks. Be sure you know how long the property has been on the market[9], and it can be worth confirming with the agent that everyone who has shown interest has viewed

---

9 On most property portals now it will tell you when the property came to market or when it was reduced in price.

the property before you make an offer. Let the agent guide you on the right time to make the first offer.

If the property has only just come on the market, then you are going to have to pay the asking price or close to it. If you have really fallen in love with the property and you do not want anyone else to buy it, then this is probably the best action to take. Sometimes, this is not the time to be smart and try to get the property more cheaply, especially if your partner is keener on the property than you!

If an attractive property comes onto the market and one that looks great value for money, where there is a shortage in the market, then you will find yourself in competition with others. If you are competitive, you may find yourself in a dangerous position. It is tempting to make sure you win at all costs. This is neither clever nor sensible unless it is your dream home. You need to be able to win while still being able to afford the property.

There are multiple different offer procedures, one being the best offer or sealed bid, which are effectively the same thing. If there are two or more people who want to offer on the same property, the agent usually uses this strategy. They will call for the best and final bids by a set date and time. There are lots of strategies you can use, including the one where we put in an offer late.

You might also want to consider putting in an offer saying that you will pay £100 more than the highest other bid. However, some agents have caught on to this trick and may not accept an offer made in this way.

Another option is to offer more than you ultimately want to pay, so you get the property off the market and get contracts issued to you rather than to other interested parties. This idea puts you in control, and you can then seek to find a problem or two with the property that could justify reducing the price to what you wanted to pay. You can always blame the poor surveyor or the valuer, saying they have down-valued the property – but they may want to see some proof of this.

If there are no legal or building problems that arise when your solicitor goes through the contract, but you still do not want to pay the price you agreed, then just say, "Sorry, I no longer wish to purchase the property". Sometimes, this can result in the agent coming back to you and asking if you would offer a reduced price. You may even want to begin the conversation by saying you want to reduce the offer. At this point, the agent will then go back to see whether the other bidder is still interested. It always amazes me how often this underbidder is no longer interested. At this point, you might get away with your request for a price reduction.

I want to stress this point, having already mentioned it before, because it is a lot more common than you might think. People often contact my team to reduce the price when purchasing a property from one of our developments or when buying an individual property. I am not suggesting you should use such underhand tactics. However, it would be remiss of me not to mention the full array of tactics at your disposal – which is my ultimate aim when writing such a book.

Alternatively, you can just put your best offer forward and hope for the best. You must be in a position to complete on the purchase as soon as possible. Some sellers tend to look at the price rather than who is the best buyer. The best buyer to my mind is far more critical to the success of the transaction. I will always take less for a property if one of the buyers can complete quicker than another. Personally, I want as much certainty that my buyer will complete the sale and be able to do so as soon as possible. I don't want to gamble with someone who is not in a position to proceed. If you have a good estate agent, they should advise you accordingly.

Consequently, if you are competing for a purchase, you must prove you can proceed quickly and that you are organised, giving you a much better chance to win without having to resort to underhand tactics, because being ready and able to proceed can make a lower offer more attractive.

FINAL OR SEALED BIDS

Final and sealed bids are really the same thing. If there is more than one person interested in the property, the agent may say they will accept final bids. You will be given a day and time to get your final submissions to the agent.

Now, of course, you will want to win the bid. One trick I sometimes use is to put my bid in late by a few minutes. If you do this, you can ask the agent, who you have worked hard to develop a good rapport with, to give you a clue as to what you need to bid. Even if that doesn't work, they are still likely to accept your bid. It is a legal requirement that all offers must be reported to the owner, and it's up to the agent to get the best price.

If the seller is sensible, they will accept the 'best' offer and this is not necessarily the 'highest' offer. It is much better to select a buyer who can proceed quickly. Therefore, it is essential to make sure you state in your bid how quickly you can proceed with the sale.

Another tactic would be to bid more than you think the property is worth and then seek to reduce this price during the sales process. This depends on how ruthless you are. However, at least with this approach, you are in control of the deal, and you have the option then of proceeding or not. The good news is that these bids are not legally binding. So you can change your mind at any point before the exchange of contracts. Although you should be prepared that even if the sellers agree to the price reduction, they may be rather annoyed.

You may be asked to pay a non-refundable deposit. I would be cautious about doing this and would certainly ask for your solicitor's advice before you so do. It could be that the owner then decides not to proceed with the sale, and you need to be assured you will get the money back in this instance. Please take legal advice.

INFORMAL TENDER

An informal tender is like a final or sealed bid. The only difference is that it's being done on a more professional, legal basis. However, it is still not legally binding. In other words, because it's informal, you will be able to change your mind and not proceed even if you are the successful bidder. Again, you may be asked to pay some sort of non-returnable or returnable deposit as a gesture of good faith. Again, please take legal advice.

FORMAL TENDER

I would advise against entering a formal tendering process, as it is legally binding. It is akin to exchanging contracts on the purchase, as you are expected to pay a full 10% deposit and to have already investigated all the legal aspects before the tender date.

Formal tenders are often used for more significant properties, such as large residential or commercial buildings. It is unlikely you will come across many formal tenders when looking to acquire a residential property. If you do, I suggest staying well clear unless you have got experience in this field. Alternatively, you should take professional advice.

CONDITIONAL AUCTIONS

I have written a book entitled Buying and Selling at Auction, which is an essential read if you are thinking of proceeding in this way.

Conditional auctions are far more prevalent in the north of England. It is like a traditional auction, as the hammer falls the purchase is conditional upon you receiving a mortgage and the legal investigations. However, there are now a number of companies offering conditional auctions across the whole of the UK and it is thus becoming a more common practice.

You may well be asked to pay a 10% deposit, please ensure that this is returnable if you do not proceed with the transaction. As the buyer, you will pay a large commission to the auctioneer, so you must be aware of the amount prior to bidding.

The auctioneers that carry out this type of auction will say that few conditional sales fall through. I find this difficult to believe, as on average,

30% of properties sold 'Subject to Contract' fall through in the UK. I can't believe this type of sale would be any different in relation to this statistic.

TRADITIONAL AUCTIONS

The traditional auction is the most common type. You will be allowed to view the properties before the auction date. On the date of the sale, you will make a bid. If you're successful, you will have to exchange contracts there and then, paying a 10% deposit and completing within 28 days.

Please do not buy a property this way without viewing it several times. Make sure your finance is in place, and that you have thoroughly assessed the legal pack. You should also have asked your solicitor to review the legal pack for you.

Having said all of this, if you are looking for a bargain property on which you can make a profit, then there is nothing wrong with buying at auction. Just remember – buyer beware! Make sure you know why the property is in the sale in the first place and that you can deal with any problems that arise, as it will likely not have had a survey.

ONLINE AUCTIONS

Online auctions have only begun in the last few years, as a new way to buy and sell property. While I was a director and shareholder of Auction House, we launched our online offering. It was a disappointing experience, in as much as it was difficult to convince buyers to commit online with such large amounts of money involved.

However, during and since the COVID-19 pandemic, online auctions have really come to the fore, as a result of there being no alternative. Requiring these types of auctions to be carried out has convinced auctioneers and the public alike that these will persist and will, most likely, continue to grow. Another reason for their increasing popularity is the reduction in costs for the auction house.

You will be given a closing time for bids. Nothing will happen until 15 minutes before the bids close. Sales are generally agreed upon the solicitor doing the legal work. However, you need to know before bidding if your offer is conditional or not.

Again, the buyer tends to pay commission to the auctioneer so please check how much and build it into your costs. Read the conditions of sale carefully and take legal advice before proceeding.

If you win the bid, from that point on it is likely to follow a similar process to that when purchasing a property, the traditional way through a local estate agent.

CHAPTER 28

MORTGAGES

REPAYMENT OR INTEREST ONLY

Whether to take out a repayment or interest-only product is a common issue surrounding mortgages. If you choose a repayment mortgage, you will pay off the whole of the sum borrowed over a set time, usually 25 years. If you select an interest-only mortgage, you will only pay the interest, and you will still owe the capital sum originally borrowed.

Everybody's personal circumstances are different. You should take the advice of your mortgage broker. Any help I offer is only generally applicable and based on my own experience. You should always seek independent advice from someone who understands your situation.

I have always found it sensible to pay off a loan as soon as possible. If you can afford to pay your mortgage in 15 years rather than 25 years, this will make a significant difference to the total amount you eventually pay. You will literally save yourself thousands of pounds because you are paying 10 years less in interest.

If you start a mortgage on a 25-year timeframe but find you can afford to pay it off early, you will need to know if there are penalties for early repayment. There are mortgage products that allow you to pay off lump sums or to reduce the number of years as you go along, and this flexibility could be useful.

There are arguments against early repayment; for instance, if you are purchasing a property that is at the top of your budget. If you have stretched your finances to buy a property, then you will want as many years as you can to pay it back. Some mortgage products run for 35 years, for instance. Also, you may be looking to buy a second or third property and so build up a property portfolio. If this is the case, you will want to keep any repayments as low as possible to maximise your return on your property.

If you are looking to create a property portfolio, an interest-only mortgage might be the best option. However, you are only able to use this strategy if the product is available to you, which is another reason to find the best mortgage broker. The payment on an interest-only product will be significantly lower, as you are not paying back any capital. The presumption is that if you are buying a second property you could sell it at the end of the term to pay back the loan.

Alternatively, an interest-only product may be linked to an endowment policy that is issued by an insurance company. So, you pay the insurance company an amount every month. The company will invest this money on your behalf, and the idea is that there will be enough money in the kitty at the end of the term to pay off the capital on your loan. However, in recent times, these investments have not performed well, and people have been left with a shortfall. Therefore, there is a risk that you will not have enough money to pay the capital at the end of the term.

If you are thinking about an interest-only mortgage, you really need to be sure how you will pay off the loan at the end of the term. If you are really stretching to buy your dream property, it might be an idea to go with an interest-only product for a period and then switch to a repayment when you are earning more money.

But remember, you should take financial advice from those qualified and certified by the Financial Conduct Authority (FCA). You can search the register of independent financial advisors to find out if your advisor is covered by the FCA.

FIXED OR VARIABLE INTEREST RATE

Another important question I am often asked is about taking out a fixed rate or a variable rate mortgage. I am not a financial advisor or mortgage broker, but I have borrowed tens of millions of pounds over 40 years, so I will speak from my experience.

There are a lot of financial institutions that offer fixed-rate mortgages. The period when the interest rate is fixed is usually between two and five years. The bank or building society is using its best judgement to assume that the interest rates will not go up. The interest rate is controlled by the Bank of England. If the economy is stable, but inflation is rising, they may increase interest rates to slow down the price rises. However, for a long time now, the Bank of England has been reluctant to put up interest rates because it can lead to people experiencing financial difficulties. This has led to a trend of particularly low-interest rates.

The lender may offer you an attractive fixed rate to encourage you to choose that. However, after the fixed period, the rate could go up considerably, as you move to a variable rate. Of course, at this point, you will have the option to change your mortgage provider. However, remember there could be a penalty for early repayment of the original loan, and this should be something you talk through with your mortgage broker. You need to discuss and weigh up the options, anticipating what might happen after whatever fixed period you are offered.

Some major banks do offer 10-year fixed-rate mortgages. However, they tend to offer such rates to large commercial organisations who need a higher level of confidence to continue investing in the future. Similarly, a lot of countries will borrow from world banks over a more extended fixed-rate period.

A fixed-rate does give you some confidence in how much you will be expected to pay over a given term, which will allow you to budget accurately. However, as stated, you should always discuss the consequences of your decision with an accredited financial advisor.

CHAPTER 29
HAVING AN OFFER ACCEPTED

When you have an offer accepted on a property, you will be excited about the potential purchase; all buyers feel the same. However, remember that this is only the start of the journey and not the finish line. There is still a massive amount of work required to drive the sale through to completion. The buying process is a team effort, so don't expect your solicitor to do it all. You will need to make a significant effort, as does the estate agent and the person selling the property, if you want a smooth sale.

THE ESTATE AGENT'S QUESTIONS

Once your offer is accepted, the estate agent will ask for the name of the solicitor you will be using for the transaction. As you now know the purchase price, you should be able to confirm a fixed price for your solicitor's services for completing the conveyancing. Please make sure you do get this fixed price, and you follow the advice from chapter one.

The estate agent will also ask if you have a mortgage agreed in principle. They will want you to prove this is the case, and you should already have this in place.

Next, if your property is sold 'subject to contract', the estate agent should investigate the chain to make sure everybody is in a position to proceed. This is commonplace, and I would be disappointed in any estate agent who failed to do this on behalf of a client.

If there is a link somewhere in the chain not yet ready to proceed, then all transactions must wait to proceed. If you haven't sold your home the estate agent is unlikely to recommend your offer to their client, even though they are legally bound to present it and will ask you to come back when you are in a position to proceed.

If you can proceed, the estate agent will then write to both sets of solicitors, sharing all the contact details of the seller and vendor. Hopefully, if the seller's solicitor is on the ball and the owner has already provided the information, they should have already drawn up the sales contract, which your solicitor will receive.

LOCAL SEARCHES

The contract, on receipt, will be accompanied by a plan of the property. With this information, your solicitor has everything required to begin the legal searches, which involves applying to the local authority. However, as these searches cost a couple of hundred pounds or so, the solicitor might wait until you have your mortgage offer before they start the searches. If you are absolutely sure of your mortgage offer, you can insist that the solicitor begins the application straightaway.

I always advise starting the searches immediately, as you may find something that you don't like. It could be that there is a road proposed within the next two years that runs close to the property or that a new development is proposed. These details could change your opinion on the purchase, making you feel negative enough to pull out. The searches can take up to a month to come back. If you apply for the searches well in advance, trying to be on the ball as a buyer, you could run into trouble as they are only valid for three months. It is possible to seek insurance for these searches, which can extend their life. However, you need to check with your lender to see if they are happy with this approach.

Whatever you decide, you need to remember that if the lending organisation is not happy with your searches, valuation, or legal work, they will not lend on the property.

HOME SELLERS' INFORMATION FORM

The home sellers' information form is sent out by the owner's solicitor for their client to complete. This document covers everything, including who supplies the gas and electricity, the last time the property was rewired, who owns the fences in the garden and if there are any outstanding disputes with neighbours. I personally hate filling in these forms, and as far as possible, I try to persuade my solicitor to do it for me. However, as much as I dislike this job, it is essential information that will likely speed up the process. Don't let this sit on your desk for even a day before you return it to the solicitor, because nothing else will happen at their end until this has been completed.

ENQUIRIES FORM

Acting for you as the buyer, your solicitor will send the enquiries form to the seller's solicitor. The enquiries form will likely ask several ridiculous questions as well as some sensible ones. No matter how silly they seem, it is essential your solicitor is satisfied with the answers given, or else they will not recommend that the property is suitable for a mortgage.

Legal work should only take about 28 days at the most, although I am aware it can take up to 3 months. It depends how promptly the owner gets the information back to the solicitor.

MORTGAGE OFFER

In a perfect world, the completion of this legal work should coincide with your mortgage offer. I am always pleased when a buyer has a mortgage offer confirmed, as I know they are close to committing to the purchase. The buyer is often excited to receive the offer, and this will normally remain valid for three months. If the remaining process takes longer than three months to draw down the funds for the purchase, you will need to reapply for the mortgage.

CHECK YOUR FINANCES

Once you get your mortgage offer, you need to double check all the costs involved in the purchase. You need to be sure that you have left nothing out. You should have enough money to pay for:

- Stamp duty
- Solicitor's fees and disbursements
- Mortgage broker fees (if applicable)
- Moving costs

The good news is that normally, you do not need to start paying the mortgage until the end of the first month living in the property. This delay in your first payment will undoubtedly help with cashflow at this point.

Although I would definitely recommend checking with your lender that this is the case, as naturally, different organisations have different policies.

CHAPTER 30
SHOULD I GET A SURVEY?

As a developer, my heart sinks when a buyer requests a survey to be undertaken. My personal view is that if you get a mortgage, any decent valuer will recommend a survey is undertaken at that point, if it is necessary. If the valuer acting on behalf of your mortgage company is happy, then on an average property in good condition, there is little point in wasting anything from £500 to £2000 on a building survey. However, my view is different if the property is in poor condition or if you are a naturally anxious person who needs the reassurance that this can provide.

There are two types of property survey, both of which are readily available through the Chartered Institute of Surveyors. The first is The Homebuyers' Report, which is carried out by a chartered surveyor; like any survey the person carrying it out must be suitably qualified. A Homebuyer's Report covers the main points, including the structure of the building, although it does not go into any great detail.

If you feel you need a more detailed survey, you could always ask them to return to complete a full structural survey. This second type of survey is comprehensive. It will identify every crack and discrepancy within the property and will likely scare you half to death. With both surveys, look to the conclusions and recommendations first. If these are mostly positive, then you haven't got too much to worry about, no matter how the whole report reads.

I know of some property buyers, those who buy a lot of houses, who will always request a survey. They do this so they can go back and renegotiate the price, using the survey as their justification for doing so. They will say, "Well, it's not me, it's my surveyor." They will then state the estimated cost for all the work, even though they would probably only undertake a small amount of what is recommended. They will also likely get it done a lot cheaper than the price they are being quoted.

If you are the seller and this strategy is used on you, it can be very frustrating and feel extremely disappointing. Although, you are now armoured with the information as to why they are doing this, which enables you to counter their revised offer.

CHAPTER 31
REDUCING THE PRICE

No one enjoys being in the position where they have to tell the seller of a property that they must reduce the price. Normally, this is the role of the estate agent once you have instructed them to do so. You may have a really good reason for needing to pay less money than was originally agreed but you cannot expect anyone to feel delighted by your reduced offer.

Most estate agents will take your request and attempt to sugar-coat this with the owner, shaping the information in a way that is easy for them to digest. However, when speaking to you, they might not be so happy, as they don't like receiving or passing on bad news, but who does? They could start by making out that this is the first time this has happened to them and attempt to make you feel guilty. However, I can assure you that this is not the case, estate agents have to deliver bad news all the time; and this is one of the reasons why the industry has a less than glowing reputation.

At the end of the day, you could argue it is business and if I offered £10,000 to anybody, who wouldn't want it? You should have a sensible, rational and genuine reason for reducing your offer. If this is the case, then it can only be the right thing to do.

One genuine reason might be that you have had a survey done and it has brought up lots of issues and problems that will cost a lot of money. This is a particularly justifiable decision if the seller did not inform you that there were problems during viewing. It is surely then only right that they agree to a reduction in price, so you can afford to put the problems right. Conversely, if you knew about the problems before the offer was made, it would be equally unfair to then demand a reduction in price.

This is the time when the excellent relationship you built up with the estate agent will pay off. The more they like you, the harder they will work to bring the deal to a satisfactory conclusion. Remember, a reduction in the price of the property will do little to the commission they earn anyway, so they will still want to see this deal through to completion.

CHAPTER 32

WHAT CAN I DO TO HELP GET A SALE THROUGH QUICKLY?

There is plenty you can do to get the sale through quickly. It is essential that you are active in driving the transaction to completion. Over the last 40 years, I can honestly say that if I hadn't driven my property deals though, a lot of them would not have happened. If I had just left it to the 2 solicitors involved, I wouldn't have done half the deals I have.

I am not criticising solicitors. My solicitor has worked for me for over thirty years. However, it takes a team to drive through the sale. There is always another solicitor on the other side of the transaction, who you hope is as good as yours, and although some are, most are not.

You have a responsibility to everyone involved in the sale to get back all the information requested as soon as possible, preferably on the same day. If your solicitor requires money upfront to get the transaction moving, then don't leave it a week or so, send them the money straightaway. The point I am making is that you are the driving force behind the sale, and an efficient and organised person will succeed at this better than those who are not.

If there is a blockage in the system, where sellers are not getting back quickly to their solicitor, you need to contact the estate agent. The agent will then chase the people in the chain and encourage them to move more quickly. If the estate agent won't or can't make this call, you need to try to make it yourself.

Also, if the solicitors on both sides are arguing, it is up to you and the other party to resolve the dispute. Some solicitors are more efficient than others. Some go into far too much detail in a transaction, slowing it down almost to a halt.

There are also solicitors who love to score points against others, letting their ego get the better of them. It is fine if it is their own property that they are buying or selling, but it should not happen when they are representing someone else. If it happens, do not let your solicitor continue with this type of behaviour. It is especially challenging, though, if both solicitors are exhibiting the same attitude. You may need to think about stopping it in whatever way possible by conceding on a few points that they are arguing about that are not essential to the transaction.

To understand whether you should concede a point or not, you should ask yourself these questions:

- Is it going to stop the building society lending me the money for the purchase?
- Is it going to stop me selling the property in the future?
- Is it going to stop me making alterations and enjoy living in the property?

Picking the right solicitor is vital, as I have stated before. Make sure they offer practical advice and action and are not ruled by ego. Instructing the right solicitor could be the difference between buying your dream home and having the transaction fall through.

Finally, to help the sale go through, you can offer to help the other party. It may be they are elderly and need assistance in organising removal vans and other aspects of moving. If there is something you can do to smooth the process, then by helping them, you help yourself.

CHAPTER 33

EXCHANGING CONTRACTS

I am now assuming you have got over all the aforementioned hurdles, you have your mortgage offer, and everybody else in the chain is in the same position too. Now you are ready to exchange contracts.

Firstly, you need to sign the contracts, which are normally sent out by post. However, I suspect that in the future, this will be modernised, perhaps allowing for e-signatures, as are already common for leases. For the process to continue, you need to sign these documents and send them back to your solicitor. It is an essential step for the exchange of contracts, and the transaction on the properties to complete. I have known people who have kept the contracts, not realising that they should send them back so the exchange can continue. I find this quite remarkable.

When you receive the contract, it will feel exciting as you are about to make your new purchase. This is what you have been working towards for the last 8 to 12 weeks.

When signed, you will need to confirm when you wish to complete and must be agreed by all parties; until then the exchange of contracts cannot go ahead.

The process of agreeing a date to move can, of course, be difficult. However, you need to remember the longer the chain, the more time it will take. It is possible to short-circuit this delay by asking the agent to ring around the other agents in the chain, seeking an agreement between them as to when the completion might take place. This is more useful than waiting for a solicitor, who can take forever to chase up the contracts.

Even though some people can be selfish and delay the process because of a birthday or a holiday, eventually everyone will agree on a completion date and the exchange can take place.

Under normal circumstances, a 10% deposit is the required amount to exchange contracts. However, this can be negotiated if needed. For instance, if you are a first time buyer who is having a 95% mortgage you will likely not have the full 10% deposit. If you are selling a property, then your deposit will likely be covered without you needing to find additional money.

After a date is agreed, solicitors will talk on the phone and verbally exchange the contract, before following up with the physical transfer of paperwork. Most solicitors like to exchange on a Friday, and in my experience if this doesn't happen it won't happen on the following Monday either!

Solicitors can leave the exchange open, which allows them to give authority to exchange any time during that day. This means that if they keep missing each other on the phone, the process will not be delayed.

Congratulations! You have now exchanged your contracts, and you have a date when the transaction will complete. You now need to make sure you get the property insured as soon as the contracts exchange, as you are technically now the owner even though you haven't completed. You should also find out the water, gas and electricity supplier, making sure the meters are read close to the moment of you moving in.

Most importantly, if you are like me, make sure you have Sky Sports organised too!

CHAPTER 34
COMPLETION DAY

When your completion date does finally arrive, you must ensure that you are completely organised. You won't be able to move into the property until you have authority from your solicitors that the monies have been transferred to the seller's solicitor.

From time to time, you will see removal vans parked outside a property with nothing happening. This is normally because the completion monies have not yet been received, and they are not allowed to unload until this is complete. It is unlikely that this payment transfer will happen before lunchtime, which can be inconvenient.

When you get the keys and open the front door, you will hope that the previous owners have undertaken a thorough clean and left everything in proper order. You will expect they have left everything that was agreed within the contract, such as carpets, curtains, and light fittings.

Try not to be disappointed if you feel the house looks different to when you viewed it. Remember, you are now seeing it without furniture. And as I mentioned earlier, the rooms will look bigger, décor will look a little more tired, and there will likely be marks where paintings have been and dents in the carpet or even wear. You might feel that you don't want the curtains and carpets. However, on the day that you move in, these will be a good starting point that you can change at a later date.

Some property owners do such a thorough job of moving out that they take lightbulbs, toilet roll holders and everything else that isn't nailed down. This might feel a little petty, as you have just paid thousands upon thousands of pounds for the house. However, it is a good idea to be prepared for this in case the seller has done this; I recommend packing these essentials in the first box you unload.

You would hope they have cut the grass and the hedges and cleaned the cooker. If they haven't, you really have no choice but to get on and do it yourself. The 'horse has already bolted' and chasing them to do jobs they should have done is almost impossible and will prove to be a lot more effort than just getting them done yourself.

Make sure you know where the stopcock, gas main pipe and fuse box are. You might need to react to an emergency in the night and regret not having located these early on.

Finally, remember it may take a few weeks to feel at home and relaxed in your new property. I am sure the thought of starting all over again with the whole buying process is difficult to contemplate, so take time and know you will feel settled soon.

ADDING VALUE TO YOUR PURCHASE

Whether you are purchasing a house, bungalow or a flat, there are ways that you can add value to your property. Whatever your circumstances, you probably should be looking to squeeze every ounce of potential value out of the purchase as you never know what the future might hold.

This is your home. I appreciate that you need to weigh up how you wish to live and the small luxuries you want to add, balanced with a desire to increase the value of the property in the long term. There are plenty of things you can do to your property for both personal benefit and as a wise commercial decision. However, there are also choices you make that could have the opposite effect, reducing the value of your property. Some expensive alterations made for personal benefit will never offer a return on the investment.

Therefore, when considering any modernisation and alteration, you will need to appeal to as many potential purchasers as you can. Anything too radical or 'brave' could be counterproductive.

A simple example would be if you have a two-bedroom flat and you knocked down a wall to have 1 larger bedroom. For you, as a couple with no desire for children, this could be an incredible luxury. However, when you come to sell it, this will reduce your property to a one-bedroom flat, which will reduce both interest and the price you are able to achieve.

Another example is where you have a reasonable sized garden but put up a large and unsightly shed that takes up most of the space; this could reduce the value of the property. The outdoor space might not have been useful to you, but for some, the size of the garden is a significant issue.

You need to spend money where it matters. One way to do this is to add a car parking space. If you can add an area to the front or rear of your home, it doesn't cost a lot to create a space and could add value to the property when it comes to resale. However, you do need to get permission from the council to add a dropped curb. You will also need to check planning permission, as you may be in a conservation area. Garages feel like an attractive addition to a house. However, few people look after the car to this degree anymore. Adding a garage to a property can be expensive, and you are unlikely to get your money back during a sale.

Inside the house, updating the kitchen and bathrooms often works well. A quality looking kitchen and bathroom will definitely aid in finding a buyer quickly. However, you can be smart with this venture and get the same look for £5000 rather than £25000, although this does depend on the house itself as well as your decisions and vision for the property.

Most kitchen carcasses are the same, meaning the only real difference between a cheap or expensive kitchen is the quality of the cupboards and worktops. Alternatively, you could just change the cupboard doors, or even paint the doors and change the handles; this can still be really effective!

If you wish to do more structural work, it seems to be very fashionable to have a large kitchen/diner. Personally, I prefer a separate dining room and drawing room to the kitchen. However, I appreciate the need to move with the times. Please also remember to take advice when making a structural changes, as you don't want to take a wall down and find it brings down half the house in the process. If there are any outbuildings connected to the main structure, these can sometimes be brought within the main accommodation and provide valuable additional space.

Ultimately, remember there is a limit to the value of any property. You can only add so much value, so you need to keep an eye on property portals, alternatively you can take advice from your estate agent to understand what the upper limit for your house will always be and take a look in their window. It is good to know the maximum value for a property like yours, as it will help you to avoid getting too carried away and overspending. Yet, if you are buying a large, detached property standing in substantial grounds, you will have more flexibility than with a small, terraced home.

CHAPTER 35
WHAT COULD GO WRONG?

It is better to be forewarned, and then you can be prepared for all possibilities. You might not be able to avoid some of the problems, but if you know they can and do happen, you can rationally deal with the aftermath.

GAZUMPING

Gazumping is the word used by estate agents to refer to being outbid by another party on a property. Even though you have agreed to buy, someone can still come along before the contracts have been exchanged and offer more. This is a trend that occurs when the housing market is buoyant, or there is a beautiful property that has come to market.

In 1997, I bred a horse and named it Gazumper. This was the time when the property market was recovering, and gazumping had started to take place again.

A small anecdote before returning to the topic of property. Gazumper became the Riding Horse Overall Champion at both The Horse of the Year Show and at the Olympia Horse Show. If you know about horses, you'll realise this is quite an achievement. Sadly, I had sold the horse by this point to someone with the talent to shape it into the champion it became. Yet, if you do some research, you will know the new owner kept the name, which makes me smile at the idea of a large proportion of the audience wondering at such an odd name for a horse.

Anyway, let's get back to what it means to be outbid by another party. My first piece of advice is definite: if you have enough money to match or exceed the offer, then increase your offer and get the property purchased. It might feel challenging to go back and offer more, but as the saying goes, 'pride comes before a fall'. It is too easy to say you won't pay more on principle. However, when you sit down in your dream home, you will be glad you went the extra mile. You may still be left with a bad taste in your mouth, but at least you'll have pushed the transaction through and secured the property for yourself. You'll also be secure in the knowledge that it is a desirable place to live, and therefore will have a good resale value if that ever becomes a reality.

I have painful experiences of refusing to match a higher offer, with my solicitor already in receipt of the sales contract waiting to be signed. On most occasions, I have matched the offer. Yet, for those that I didn't, I look back now with regret. Remember, you are still the one in the driving seat, as you are the one with the contract. The seller, by accepting a different offer, would have to start the process again with a new buyer. Therefore, matching the bid should be enough.

ADVERSE SURVEY REPORT

When you first receive the report, the best thing to do is to take a bit of time to think about the problem before making a decision. Avoid getting on the phone straight away to the agent or the owners, leave yourself some time to consider the consequences. I always read the recommendations first, as this will give you a more balanced view than scanning through each individual item. You should talk to the surveyor who has written the report, as sometimes the issues can sound worse written down that they are in reality.

After you have had time to digest the report and seek further feedback, you should then speak to the agent. Ask them if it's acceptable to send a builder to the property to get an estimate for the required work. You have some right to expect this access, as these are problems that you didn't know when you made the offer, rather than the jobs you felt had to be done anyway. The agent will seek permission from the owners for a visit from the builder.

If you don't have a builder, you might want to ask the estate agent if they could recommend anyone. It is also possible the seller of the house knows a builder who they feel happy to organise to visit the home. The agent likely has contacts in most trades, including those who can rectify damp or problems with timber.

If you contact the owner, you may wish to ask if they will go some way to cover the extra costs that have now become clear. They may be willing to reduce the price of the house substantially to help cover the costs. It is up to you if you want to get involved in such a negotiation. The agent may be willing to help you by discussing this with the owner, as they want the sale to complete. To be fair, the owner wants a deal too, so is likely to be willing to negotiate with you, as the problems you have uncovered have either come up before or will come up again with a future purchaser.

As your whole chain needs to complete on the same day, you need to remember there might be a lot of people hoping you and the seller can come to a compromise.

THE SELLER CAN'T FIND A PROPERTY

A seller unable to find an onward property is a significant problem, especially if the owners are old and looking to downsize to a smaller property. If they have lived in their home for a long time, it can be quite a wrench to leave. There can also be a lot of furniture and a lifetime of belongings to get rid of before they can move somewhere smaller. All this can be quite daunting for any age group but particularly for the older generation, and equally as sad.

Always try to find out if they have children and consider contacting them to see if they can help move things along. The children are usually the driving force behind the sale, hoping to see their parents settled. Often, they want them closer to where they live, so are generally willing to help.

If they are not elderly, they may be just struggling to find what they are looking for. Equally, they could be disorganised or not fully committed to selling in the first place if they don't really want to move. You need to get a feel for this when you are viewing the property. You should try to judge the level of seriousness of the vendor and the likelihood that they will complete the transaction.

You can get an early feel for this by asking the estate agent if the property has been on the market before. If the agent's answer is yes, then I would be dubious as to whether they are going to be fully committed to selling this time too.

TEMPORARY ACCOMMODATION

If you are the person in the sales chain that is holding up the exchange and completion for others, you may consider moving into temporary accommodation to move the transaction along.

Moving into temporary accommodation is a radical and brave thing to do. You will be hoping that this move will help you eventually purchase your dream home. However, there are a few risks when choosing such a strategy. Firstly, you will have taken the pressure off the people who are selling you their property. They will no longer feel any great rush to find an alternative property. Reducing the stress might be all the room they need to make a better go at finding their house; however, it could also serve to help them relax too much.

If you do choose temporary accommodation, the easiest option is to rent a property for six months. There is an obvious cost involved in doing this – not just the rent but the additional moving costs. Yet, the upside is that you are no longer in a chain; therefore, you become a desirable buyer to both estate agents and to the owners. However, you run the risk of the property market increasing in value while you are waiting for the perfect home to land in your lap.

Rather than rent, you could always move in with friends or with your family. If you are a couple, this can be a stressful option. I would imagine moving in with parents could have lots of undesirable consequences. Even if you stay with a friend, how long will they stay friends if you are still living with them six months later?

If temporary accommodation is a means of bridging a short gap, then it should be fine. Therefore, you may want to get a commitment from the owners of the property that they will definitely sell it to you first. You may be able to exchange contracts with a delay on completion, allowing them enough time to find alternative accommodation. If they are not prepared to do so, then ask for some sort of option that gives you the first chance to buy the property at an agreed price. This is the moment when you need an outstanding solicitor.

THE CHAIN BREAKS

Chain breaks are common, and if you are in the unfortunate position to have multiple links, but have the option to, I would always recommend to go with the shortest chain even if the offer is slightly less. Always go for the best buyer rather than simply the best price. The longer the chain, the greater the risk. It is challenging to get everybody ready to exchange at the same time and complete on the same day.

A sales chain of, let's say, 6 properties often breaks. If someone loses a buyer, there are really only two options. Firstly, you can wait for the broken link in the chain to find another buyer. Obviously, this can take a long time – though it might be sped up if they agree to reduce the price. Secondly, you can choose to put your house back on the market, with the acknowl-edgement that if the chain comes back together, they can make the offer on your property again. This choice allows you to get two bites at the cherry to move the transaction forward. However, the risk here is that you dishearten your current buyer and they decide to look for a new property too. Yet, if they are no longer in a position to proceed anyway, you are unlikely to lose much by doubling your chances of a sale.

DIVORCE

At the time of writing, approximately 42% of marriages end in divorce which does of course impact the housing market. As previously mentioned, it is often said that the transaction of purchasing or selling a property is only second to divorce in terms of stress, and often the two go hand in hand, compounding the emotional challenge. Therefore, it is very important when buying a property from, or selling a property to, a divorced couple that the ex- or soon to be ex-spouse is also committed to the sale, the price and the timescale. There is little that is more frustrating than when one of the parties refuses to sign in order to exchange contracts, thus not allowing the other person to move on to their new property.

BRIDGING LOANS

Whilst all this advice about problems that may occur during the transaction might be a little disheartening, there is a potential solution: seeking out a bridging company. These institutions are usually small banks that lend money for short periods at high interest, offering what is known as a bridging loan.

If you have enough equity in your property (cash left over after you have paid off your mortgage), they may lend you all the money to complete the purchase of your new property. You can then move while your old one is still on the market.

This is not without risk. It could take you a long time to sell the property and, in the meantime, you are racking up considerable interest. Potential buyers may also work out that you have taken out a bridging loan and may use this to leverage a lower price on your property. Remember, you should always take advice from a qualified, independent financial advisor to check that you are not overstretching yourself.

CONCLUSION

Hopefully you have already enjoyed reading this book and not just looked at the conclusion first, which is what I advise you to do with the property surveys!

There seems to be a common denominator throughout all the books I write and the advice I give at seminars about property and it is this, be organised.

If you remember, I started the book by suggesting that you get all your professional advisors on board before you start looking to purchase your first, second, or even third home. Whether you have a house to sell or are a first-time buyer, the organisation and discipline of knowing how much you can spend and who is going to legally advise you is essential for successful outcome.

The process is the same when I'm developing my property deals, you need to know how much you can spend and you need to have the best legal advisor you can find, not the cheapest!

My stepdaughter and her partner have recently gone through the process of selling one property and buying a new one. She very kindly said that she's been spoiled by having me advise them through the process to make it as smooth and stress free as possible.

I asked her the one thing throughout the whole process that made a difference and the answer was, the solicitor.

Now she used the solicitor that I work with for the last 30 odd years so I'm glad she said that, it looks like I made a very good decision all those years ago to start working with Mark Hayward!

But the contrast between Mark and the solicitor the buyer of their property used was immense. All the usual problems occurred, not being able to get hold of them when required, not returning calls and not getting on with the work as quickly as they could, and so on...

What really scares me about some of the solicitors is how many times over the years they have let down their clients to such an extent that people have lost their dream home through their lack of effort and, in some cases, just poor advice.

I was recently asked the question, probably because of my age, "What won't you miss about your property career?" And my only thought that was the time it takes between when a buyer is found for a property and when it's finally sold.

I think I said earlier that I still get a thrill every time I exchange contracts on a property whether I'm buying or selling because it takes such an effort to do so unless it's in an auction.

Governments over the years have tried try to speed up this process but due to a number of factors it's incredibly hard to do.

And, of course, it's sometimes totally out of your hands however good your solicitor is, if the solicitor on the other side of the transaction is not competent or too busy, holding up your sale or purchase in this way can lead to grave consequences. Of course, they will still charge you, probably a rather large fee for their poor effort.

If you are able to recommend a solicitor that you know is good to the person on the other side of the transaction, I would certainly do this. I appreciate that shouldn't be the case and that you could argue it has nothing to do with you who another person choses as their solicitor, but I can tell you it does.

I hope you've managed to take information away with you from reading this book that will help you have a smoother and more successful acquisition, sale or both.

I'm sure you're pleased that you haven't done it almost 4000 times like I have, and still counting!

If you have got the property bug and want to do more than just own your own home, then I'm sure my other property books will be of use to you.

It just remains for me to wish you the smoothest move possible.